TONY
Our Journey Together

TONY

Our Journey Together

Carolyn A. Koons

1817

Harper & Row, Publishers, San Francisco

Cambridge, Hagerstown, New York, Philadelphia
London, Mexico City, São Paulo, Sydney

First Harper & Row paperback edition published in 1985.

Library of Congress Cataloging in Publication Data

Koons, Carolyn A.
  TONY, OUR JOURNEY TOGETHER.

  1. Koons, Antonio Hernandez Sanchez. 2. Koons, Carolyn A. 3. Christian
biography—United States. 4. Adoption—Law and legislation—Mexico.
5. Children, Adopted—United States—Biography. I. Title.
BR 1700.2.K6 1983   280'.4[B]   83-48432
ISBN 0-06-064762-0
ISBN 0-06-064764-7 (pbk.)

---

85 86 87 88 89 10 9 8 7 6 5 4 3 2

DEDICATED TO

My son Tony:

For all the years of pain you have suffered.

For all life's lessons you have learned and are still learning.

For not giving up and for all that you have become as a young man for Christ. And especially for being my son, which has helped me to grow and change for you. Tony, you have changed my life.

And to all the Tonys who surround us—whether you be that person we read about in the newspaper, an acquaintance, a close friend, or a family member.

And to the little bit of Tony in all of us.

May God help us let go of the pain and the memories of the past. He cares for us. God will reach down into the depths of our soul and "change our life." He has a special journey for all of us . . . if we will just let Him.

Acknowledgments

To—

Azusa Pacific University, which has been a dynamic influence in my life over the last twenty years. To my extended family of friends at the university, for their encouragement and help, nurturing and faith, I owe a tremendous debt. For without them this book could not have been written. I'm especially grateful to them for affirming me in my commitment to Tony and contributing through much encouragement to our successful journey as mother and son and to our obedience to God.

To—

Barbara Fraley, my close friend, who shares with me the memories of that first day in the Mexican prison when we discovered Tony. Through the years she has helped me maintain—and sometimes regain—my perspective so that I could recognize the lessons that I needed to learn as Tony and I grew together. She also helped me outline and edit the story with keen insight into how my past related significantly to my life with Tony.

To—

Tami Files, who was a constant source of encouragement and support to me in writing. When the thought of putting our lives into writing terrified me, she dragged me out to a desert cabin and all but held my hand through the first stages of writing. Tami was still quietly supportive when we began editing and added valuable insights in that process.

To—

Virginia (Ginny) Churchill, especially, who spent hundreds of hours helping me to write, clarify, think through, question, edit, and rewrite the book. With me she shared inspiration and insight, sprinkled richly with a good sense of humor. She was my right arm and shadow throughout the whole writing process—an adventure in itself!

To—

Linda Tavenner, my wonderfully faithful secretary, who without complaint typed day after day the roughest of drafts and tediously retyped the numerous drafts that confused us all.

To—

And, finally, Roy M. Carlisle, my editor at Harper & Row San Francisco, a true professional who believed in me and made it possible for Tony and me to share our story. Patience and sensitivity on his part made my adventure with writing a positive and challenging experience.

TONY
Our Journey Together

Chapter One

Antonio's five-year-old imagination made fancy cars and heavy-duty trucks of the sticks he pushed through the dust. As waves of heat rose from the ground and a hot breeze carried smells of rotting garbage and sewage into his face, Antonio played on, oblivious. "Vroom, vroom," he revved a motor as the voices inside grew louder. Then the baby started crying, muffling the angry words of his mother and Jose, his stepfather. He put down his car and sat back expectantly. After a moment, Jose came to the door and roared angrily, "Antonio, Antonio!" How he hated to leave his play already. It had been days since he'd been able to escape the many duties assigned him as oldest of five children.

In response to Jose, Antonio went to the doorway of his dilapidated home, scarcely a shack, in the poorest hillside area of Tijuana, Mexico. He absorbed the familiar scene. His mother, her eyes red and swollen, sat on the bed while Jose paced angrily. From the cradle hanging above the bed, Jose grabbed the squalling baby and shoved him into Antonio's arms, "Shut him up!"

Relieved to be let off without a confrontation, Antonio took his baby brother and scurried toward the door as the fight resumed. A sharp slap and his mother's cry brought him to an abrupt stop. He stood and watched, riveted by fear, as Jose beat his mother brutally. Antonio cried out and Jose looked up, noticing the boy's presence. Further enraged by the look of fear and judgment in Antonio's eyes, he lunged at him. Antonio had seen this look of rage before and knew for certain that he should run for his life. He cautiously laid the baby down and hurdled the obstacle course of garbage and piles of junk in his backyard to the nearby lumberyard. Shouting and panting on Antonio's heels, Jose nearly caught him, but Antonio scurried nimbly up a woodpile and down the other side. With only a second to spare before his stepfather rounded the corner, he burrowed beneath an overhanging edge.

Breathless and foiled, Jose stood inches from the boy's hiding place. Antonio froze and watched his stepfather's restless scan of the lumberyard then slumped with relief as Jose walked away.

Antonio didn't feel safe enough to crawl out until after dark. He knew that he couldn't go home, so he walked aimlessly through the pitch black alleys and streets. Hunger urged him home, but fear kept him drifting. Suddenly a police car pulled up behind him and two officers approached. He was frightened, but they were kind and finally convinced him to let them take him home.

As the police car drove away from his home Antonio realized his mistake. Backing into the corner of the room, he cried out in fear as Jose thundered toward him. He was beaten nearly to death, then chained to the leg of his bed, where he lay on the floor for three days. Occasionally his stepfather came in and threw cold water on him, threatening to kill him if he ever talked to the police again.

Several days later, Antonio was once again playing in the backyard. He heard a thud from the house, and a whimper. Had the baby fallen from his crib again? Antonio ran into the house. His parents stood over the baby, who was sprawled lifeless on the floor, blood dripping from the back of his head. Beside him lay a baseball bat.

Antonio wanted to run to his baby brother, to hold and comfort him, but Jose blocked his path. "Is he all right?" Antonio asked, "Did he fall?"

"His head is cracked!" his mother said nervously. Then, in sudden anger, she grabbed Antonio and shook him violently. "What have you done to your brother?" she asked.

Jose pushed Antonio toward the bleeding baby. "You hit him," he yelled harshly.

As Antonio turned to deny the accusation, Jose knocked him to the ground. "You hit him in the head with that bat."

Antonio stared at the bat, unable to deny that it was stained with blood. Then he inched away from Jose, who continued to scream accusations. Gradually his mother's agitation grew, and she joined the screaming.

Antonio looked for an escape. Seizing his opportunity, he flew across the bed and out the door to take refuge with a neighbor—an old woman.

For fear of being found by the police and returned home, Antonio stayed with the old woman and hid beneath her bed most of the time. The sight of his baby brother's cracked head and the fear of being found by his stepfather made him too sick to eat. The first and second day passed and he began to relax; but on the third day Jose pulled up in his old pickup, a child's casket and bunches of flowers in the back. Jose rolled down his window and yelled up at the house, "Antonio Hernandez Sanchez: you killed your baby brother. May you burn in hell forever!"

The next day a car stopped in front of the old woman's shack. Terrified, Antonio hid under the bed. He heard a muffled conversation, then watched as two men's feet came to either side of the bed. Soon the old woman began coaxing him to come out. "These nice men will take care of you," she promised. She'd protected him and become his friend. Surely he could trust her, he reasoned.

He came out, reluctantly, relieved that the men didn't grab him. Cautiously he followed them to the car. Once inside, however, he noticed a radio and gun in the front seat. From the car window Antonio's familiar neighborhood melted into strange territory, and panic grew as he tried to imagine what might become of him. Later, his worst fears were confirmed when they threw him into a small, crowded cell at the men's prison.

Chapter Two

Hundreds of kids of high school and college age scurried around in every direction carrying sleeping bags, suitcases, tents, outdoor P.A. systems, and mountains of food. Everyone worked together, and our canvas village, with a population of five hundred, quickly took shape. It was quite primitive: rows of tents, each touching, covered a dusty field. Some years it rained and then muddy tents covered a muddier field, but this year it was hot—really hot.

The thrill of seeing old friends mounted as each college and church team arrived. For some, this was the fifth Easter week they had come to this tiny mission station at Ejido Cuernavaca, located twenty miles below Mexicali (a border town in Mexico just below Calexico, California).

I watched as a huge, lumbering water truck bumped across the field delivering the first of our drinking water. Our tent city would require three truckloads daily. Supply trucks had arrived two days earlier, and ovens, grills, tables, thousands of paper cups and plates, cases of canned fruit and peanut butter —literally hundreds of items—had been delivered, ready for our arrival. Assured that my dependable student staff had everything under control, I retired to my quarters—a well-used fifteen-foot trailer I referred to as the "Little Hilton."

I spent a few minutes arranging my personal belongings, then stretched out across my bed to steal a quick nap. This one week with Mexicali Outreach was the highlight of my year, and I'd had very little sleep the week before making sure every detail was in order. My staff members tease me about my endless lists, but they love me anyway. We would soon be called to dinner, and an excited frenzy would begin that would last for the next seven days. My body was dead (a good kind of tired), but my mind was in full gear. I loved these kids and their eager enthusiasm. I believed in them and couldn't wait to see each team put into practice the skills I'd been teaching them throughout the year—I knew this week would profoundly affect many lives.

I closed my eyes and thought about Azusa Pacific University's Mexicali Outreach program and its effect on my own life. The face of the late Dr. Cornelius Haggard, a dear and dedicated man of God, came to mind. As president of APU, Dr. Haggard had addressed the student body weekly. I remembered one chapel hour especially vividly. On the subject of missions, he challenged the students to a commitment:

"You've heard about missions all over the world, but we have foreign missions in our own backyard. Thousands of migrant workers are in camps only a few miles from our university; Mexico, with its poverty and unemployment, is only a few hours away. The needs of many people close by are great, and you, as students, can do something about it. What are *you* going to do?"

Dr. Haggard was right: we *could* do something to help. At nineteen, I was a student and part-time teaching assistant; I was ready to conquer the world. A handful of other eager students and I went to migrant camps near the Mexican border during the Christmas break, with the university's blessing. The experience so challenged and moved us that we prepared a multimedia presentation on our return and shared it with the other students during a chapel hour. Our enthusiasm spread across campus: that Easter break I led another group of students to Mexico, and we've made at least two trips each year since then. Within a few years, the program expanded to include young people from church youth groups near the university, and then from the entire West Coast. By the third year, the program involved five hundred energetic young people of high school and college age.

A strong core of gifted individuals evolved as the leadership base and eventually became a close-knit family unit. One of these is Pastor Ron Cline. He can make you feel you've been hugged without even touching you. His warmth and creativity have always made him a favorite among the students. Formerly dean of students at the university, he is now a full-time missionary in Equador and flies all the way from Quito to direct our chapel time and give us spiritual guidance.

It's hard not to love our head cook, Forrest Pershall. Each year he drives all the way from Colorado with his family to organize and prepare thousands of individual meals. Always smiling, Forrest is a constant source of encouragement for his kitchen staff and the entire camp.

John and Barbara Fraley, close personal friends, add depth and continuity to every aspect of the program.

And finally, there's the student director—not a permanent position, since students have a way of graduating. David Johnson was the present incumbent, now in his third year. Barely older than many of the participants, still he was a confident, effective leader. Best of all, he spoke Spanish fluently, having been born in Latin America to missionary parents.

A sturdy knock shook the Little Hilton, rousing me from my sleepy reflections, and a familiar deep mellow voice called from outside—"Hey Koons, shake your bones and get out here! I came all the way from Quito for dinner with you!"

"Hey, yourself," I yelled, "I need all the beauty rest I can get." I stumbled out the door, glad for his bear-hug greeting that broke my fall. Ron was a long-time friend and co-laborer and added immeasurably to Mexicali Outreach. Good times seem to follow him around.

"Starved?" I asked. "Let's eat and talk a bit."

"You bet," he said and led the way to our outdoor dining area. It was a good plan but poorly timed. The next two hours were like a reception at Grand Central Station—with me as hostess. Once again I realized my life was rich with friends, not just lots of people, but real, committed friends. I've never been known for my reserve or lack of enthusiasm, but tonight I was really cooking.

The last of our team arrived at 6:30 P.M. Ron and I dumped our paper plates and cups into the fire pit as we crossed the camp to greet John and Barbara Fraley. I started yelling before they stopped their van. "Glad to see you guys! I was beginning to worry. You're going to have to pay Forrest big bucks for a late dinner." We hugged as only old friends do, then laughed about being hot and sweaty already.

John brought us up to date as he threw sleeping bags and suitcases from the roof of his van. "We already paid big bucks for dinner in town. Actually, we've been down all afternoon trying to get a permit from the men's prison for a basketball team tomorrow."

Knowing the chances of getting into a Mexican prison, I sympathized. "Too much red tape, huh?"

With a triumphant "ta da," Barbara pulled a white envelope from her pocket. "Do the Fraleys ever give up? Now how about a reward? We're dying of thirst!"

Ron burst in, "You're always dying of something, Barb, but you're right, you deserve a reward!"

"It's time for our staff meeting," I added. "We'll get you something and you can tell everyone about the permit."

Abruptly, Barbara was serious, "I wonder if our kids are ready for what they'll see at the prison?" Then she turned to me. "Carolyn, you look preoccupied. Are you ready for the meeting?"

"Sure, I just have some things on my mind."

The mission station we use for our base in Mexico is a tiny building made adequate only by ingenuity. The small kitchen, a marvel of organization, was piled—to the ceiling in places —with supplies for the week. The tiny storeroom was jammed from floor to ceiling. A small room adjacent to the kitchen, our staff headquarters, buzzes with activity. Here each team must check in and out at the window, picking up their film strips, projectors, literature, and sack lunches before heading out to their assigned Mexican villages for the day. At the center of this little room is a well-worn table and too few chairs, but the staff somehow managed to crowd in, resting their bodies on chairs, boxes, and even the floor.

"I found them," Dave huffed as he came through the door. His arms were wrapped around a large box that he dropped on the table. He began pulling out T-shirts marked Mexicali Staff and tossing them around the table.

"These are sharp, Carolyn. This year, we'll be able to tell our good-looking staff from our good-looking campers!"

I glanced over the agenda in my open notebook. Neat little lists, arrows, all kinds of meticulous graffiti and check-off boxes, covered the page.

Looking up, I said, "You're all smart and good-looking." Everyone laughed and kidded around. "Now, let's get to work," I said. They were ready for me and I was ready for them. I flipped through a volume of material with dispatch.

Then I closed my folder and tapped my pen on my teeth, stalling before I continued. Except for the flies buzzing around the room and the moths flapping against the light, the room was quiet. Finally, I jumped in and said, "You've done it again —you're first class! I really appreciate all your work—everything's covered, and this week is going to be fantastic once again. In fact, I have a feeling this is going to be the best Mexicali Outreach ever!

"I know you've all worked your tails off and we need to turn in early, but I must tell you something, something rather personal. I'm not going to cry, so don't get nervous." They chuckled.

"For some time now I've felt restless, and more than a little dissatisfied, so I've taken a long, hard look at my life these last few weeks; I've looked back in order to look forward."

Hardly able to look at the faces of my friends for fear I'd cry, knowing that I had their complete attention and concern, I forced the rest out.

"As a child I did everything I could think of to earn love and acceptance." I swallowed, then said flatly, "I wasn't very successful, so I changed my tactics; the more rejection I felt, the *worse* I behaved. It was just as though I'd decided that if my world treated me as if I were bad, I'd *show* them what bad really meant. In time, all I knew was how to get into trouble. Inside, I was really lonely, and my frantic search for comfort constantly got me in trouble."

As I spoke I wondered if anyone listening could really imagine how desperately lonely and unhappy my childhood had been.

"But then, when I was a junior in high school, I faced something that utterly contradicted my whole defensive lifestyle. Someone told me that, in spite of what I did and what others thought of me, *God loved me.* God's love was so clear to me, so real, that I decided to love him too, and live the rest of my life in respect to him."

I wanted to be really clear to my listening friends, so I continued. "I mean, the first source of real love I knew was God, and I decided to return that love by making him the most important concern of my life. As days and weeks went by, I found his acceptance was so contrary to the rejection I'd come to expect that I couldn't deny him. He changed my life around. I gave in to him without a single reservation."

Feeling on safer ground, my voice became steadier. "From that day on, my life took on a new meaning. The emptiness of rejection was being replaced by committed friendships like ours." I smiled at my frank openness, so unlike I had been when growing up, and went on. "And God has helped me to accomplish things beyond my dreams: teaching at the university, organizing Mexicali Outreach—and loving every minute of life.

"But God, because he loved me, did more than change circumstances in my life—he changed *me.* I guess I feel as if he's been preparing me for something special; after all, I'd gone to some pretty dark and bitter places in my heart as a child, and he'd totally transformed my life. In a really personal way, I know exactly what we're going to be able to offer the people here in Mexicali by offering them that same life-changing love. Do you know what I mean?"

I watched them smile and nod. Knowing they were with me, I finished.

"I want this year's Mexicali Outreach to be the greatest one ever, and I think it can be. I want this experience to touch everyone here, of course, but I have a *personal* goal as well:

I'm praying that God will use this week to help me be more receptive to his will.

"So tonight I'm saying before all of you: I'm ready for whatever God has in store for me; I'm ready for this week."

Dave took my hand and gave it a squeeze. I felt other hands on my shoulders, communicating support. "We're with you, Carolyn," said Barb. "We're with you all the way."

In spite of my promise, I wiped away tears.

Chapter Three

"Great breakfast, Forrest. You fed five hundred people in an hour, that's almost ten a minute. Not bad." He was already smiling. Forrest was doing the impossible. Our kitchen facilities were meager—two large grills, a long-retired Hot Point stove, and a well-chipped portable sink/cupboard unit, 1948 vintage.

As David came through the kitchen door, Forrest handed him a large ice chest, "Here's your lunch, and don't come crying to me if those guys in the prison eat it all up."

"Thanks, Forrest. I'll guard it with my life."

By this time Barb was in the doorway and predicted that the basketball team would eat the whole thing before ten. I caught her eye from across the room. A short night's sleep behind us, we were both charged with the excitement and promise of the day ahead. "Morning, Barb," I hollered. "Can you believe we're really going inside a Mexican prison?" I was eager, but the responsibility of taking the students into such uncertainty weighed heavily on me. We had heard a lot about the prison system in Mexico, but we didn't really know what to expect.

With great care, I hand-picked the team that would go to the prison. I began with the Fraleys, Barbara and John; they had obtained the permit for our outreach into the prison and were busy informing me of the expectations and procedures we would encounter. I hadn't forgotten that sports was the grounds on which permission to visit had been granted, so I asked six members of the APU varsity basketball team to go with us. We also had some excellent music groups at Outreach; I asked a group of three musicians, with their exceptional pianist, Danny Barker, to join us. I also needed Amelia, a vivacious missionary in her late forties, to come along. She is indispensably versatile—born in Mexico, she lives in the United States with her American husband, Horace. She knows both cultures as well as both languages. Amelia and her husband founded the Cuernavaca mission where we camp, and they coordinate all of the village and mission contacts throughout the valley for our teams during Easter week.

Of course, David Johnson, my student director, always has a place on my team. And to complete the group, my good friend and past youth minister, Louie Files, who had been instrumental in my own Christian conversion. He added a spark to the group that everyone appreciated.

During the eighteen-mile ride from our camp in Cuernavaca to the prison in downtown Mexicali, we planned a simple program and tried to prepare ourselves for what was to come. The basketball team wondered what would happen to them if they won; David wisely suggested, "I think you'd better be sensitive to these men if you want to be invited back."

In spite of our preparations, we weren't ready for the extremely intimidating atmosphere of the men's prison. On the instruction of the guards at the front desk, we emptied our pockets. Then we were led into two separate rooms—men and women—and roughly frisked. Having thus assured themselves we were harmless, the guards finally led us through a series of locked gates and doors into the heart of the prison compound.

Thirty-three years old, independent, and quite confident about taking care of myself, I felt vulnerably feminine as we entered the main corridor of the prison. A handful of prisoners were congregated here; our presence broke their boredom, and they came alive. They looked at us as though we were stark naked; all four of the women on the team felt molested, I'm sure. Long, narrow blocks of cells ran at right angles to this main corridor and echoed with the noise of blaring radios and the coarse laughter and jeers of the prisoners in the gang cells. We'd heard they jammed sixty or more men into cells built to house twenty. It seemed as if hundreds of arms hung out of the bars, holding mirrors to get a fleeting glance of us gringos, especially the females. Sensing our insecurity, the guys on the team encircled us protectively.

Barbara's dark eyes flashed and her silky dark brown hair swung in a lively manner as she turned toward the commotion. "Do you think they're yelling at us? Do you think they know we're here?" Now the prisoners were banging their cups on the bars so loudly that she couldn't hear my answer. I nodded affirmatively, and she rolled her eyes. Barbara's expressions spoke volumes.

We continued through another series of locked, barred doors until we were finally ushered outside onto the cement basketball court. Rising from the court's perimeter were still more prison cells. These cells were for the privileged, who paid well for their accommodations. Each cell boasted a tiny, barred window overlooking the courtyard. As if reaching for freedom, the prisoners poked their arms out the windows, some waving them around frantically.

The air was intensely hot and very still. At first we moved in a clump down the court, then began to spread out a bit. Tilting her head toward the wall, Barb sighed, "The shade looks great, but those arms—I can almost feel them around my neck!" She mockingly throttled herself. Her humor was a relief; this place was so dreary!

I looked at the weird, snaky-looking arms crammed through the bars, then raised my eyes up to the roof. Armed guards patrolled the rooftops, and their threatening rifles were aimed in our direction. I thought I could see their fingers on the triggers—and that didn't make me feel any more comfortable. I wished they'd put their rifles down—or at least point them the other way.

Just then the door flew open and the prison basketball team piled through, commanding the court. From their windowed cells, the prisoners erupted with shouts and cheers for their team. Their fickle loyalty was not impressive—we knew that they frequently stabbed each other for trivial offenses.

Our uniformed basketball team mingled quite comfortably with the prison team and gave each member a uniform. They were obviously thrilled and immediately pulled off their smelly shirts, revealing bruises, scars, and wounds. Tattoos covered large areas of their bodies and stood out like maps of their lives. I prayed silently that we could give these men some encouragement and hope.

The whistle blew and several of us hastily jumped off the court to avoid being trampled. This was great—guards and prisoners alike were totally involved, all bellowing and screaming with excitement.

The rapid movement of bare feet on a concrete basketball court caught our "gym-trained" team off guard. The prison team made the first basket, and everyone cheered and laughed —especially the prisoners. This game was going to be a little tougher than we'd thought. But at least we had everyone's attention on the court, including the guards with the rifles.

We weren't sure who was keeping score or watching the clock. But whenever one of the teams called for the score, the prison team was always ahead by one. We looked at each other and grinned. The idea was not so much to win as to simply open up a means of communication with the prisoners and build a foundation for the future through the fun of sports.

At halftime, we gathered the men around, and the music group sang a few songs in Spanish. Smiles—some toothless— testified to the inmates' delight. They swayed in time with the music, and the prison's chaplain nodded encouragement when the men asked for "just one more." Several from our group shared a few words about their faith in God. David interpreted for them, then read some Bible verses and prayed. Throughout all this the prisoners sat with rapt attention. It was exciting and encouraging to be so well received.

By the time the second half started, much of the tension had dissipated, and a spirit of friendliness prevailed. The game finally ended amid exuberant cheers, and the officials announced the score: Prison team 67, Gringos 66. David flashed me a knowing smile. The team members shook hands, and some actually embraced. This was one game that no one minded losing.

Taking advantage of this mellow mood, our team quickly spread out among the prisoners. During the game I'd noticed a prisoner lying on a low, rickety gurney off to one side of the court. I decided to go talk to him. *"Como se llama?"* I ventured.

"My name is Curt," he said in English. Peering seriously at me, he continued, "Thanks for coming, and thanks for what your teams said out there. I really needed some encouragement." His voice drifted off.

I judged Curt to be nearly forty, but it was hard to tell. His thick red hair hung in a sweaty mass of curls that almost concealed his eyes, which darted around furtively. He was obviously nervous about being seen talking with me. The poor man looked grotesque: A thick plaster cast began at his chest and encased him to his toes. His legs were awkwardly bowed in the shape of a wishbone; only a small, filthy towel concealed his genitals, and he was otherwise naked. The cast was old and cut open in places, exposing a terribly shriveled leg and two surgical wounds that drained repulsively. His misery completely subdued my spirit. Quietly I asked, "Why are you here?"

Succinctly, he told me the circumstances of his imprisonment—a tragic story. He had been a school teacher and pilot, wanting to make some quick money for his family. Attempting to fly drugs across the border, he was caught and shot down.

I crouched on the ground beside the gurney and didn't speak for several minutes. At last, I asked him, "How long is your sentence?"

"I don't know. I've been here for eighteen months, and my case hasn't even come to trial." His body sagged with discouragement. "May I send a message with you to the States?" His voice became thick with emotion. "Please, tell my friends—tell everyone—not to do something dumb like I did. I've ruined my life. I've lost my job, my wife, my family, my leg, everything! I deserve exactly what I've got. Please, warn them!" He struggled to control his emotions, then nodded to a Mexican nearby, who quickly wheeled him away. I noticed just a slight wave of his hand.

"Good-bye, Curt." As I watched him leave, the prison's chaplain approached from behind me.

"Senorita Koons," he said, "if you have time today, will you please visit the boys' prison, too? I can make the arrangements." His kind face pleaded with me. I'm sure I had a dumb look on my own face, but I couldn't believe he was telling me that there was a boys' prison. Maybe he meant younger men.

"Boys' prison? I've never heard that there was a prison for boys."

He nodded gravely, "Yes, there is a prison for boys. I've served there, as well as here, for many years. Two hundred and fifty boys, maybe more, ages five through seventeen, are held there year round. If you leave right now, I can get your team in to see them before they're locked up for the afternoon. I've done my best, but these boys are starved for love. Absolutely anything you could do would help. Your team could have a great ministry there too."

David had overheard part of this conversation. "Carolyn, we're finished here for now; we've got enough time if the team has enough energy left."

The team and staff voiced my thoughts: "How can we *not* go?" I nodded my consent.

A smile relieved the chaplain's grimness. "I'm on my way," he announced. "I'll go ahead to make sure you get through the guards."

"Boys' prison," I muttered to myself as we made our way out through the now-familiar series of barred doors. "Surely the boys' prison couldn't be anything like this one!"

Chapter Four

The first leg of our trip from the city prison was easy, but leaving the city and the paved road promised to provide adventure. I couldn't wait. I loved this kind of day; it was grueling, but I felt intensely alive.

Billows of dust followed the van as we drove farther south into the rich farmlands of the Mexicali valley. The chaplain had given directions to the boys' prison, but we found them very misleading. Then I remembered that Amelia knew everything about Mexico. "Don't you know the way to the prison, Amelia?"

"No, I'm sorry, Carolyn. I've heard about it, but I've never been there."

As directed, we religiously tried to follow the canal road, once nearly plunging into the canal itself. Our singing group's practice session degenerated into a restless nap, and our sweaty basketball team got smellier.

I became restless myself. We couldn't find the prison. Would we be too late? Had the chaplain given up and gone home? I noticed that the gas tank registered less than a quarter full; things were getting desperate. Oh well, I grinned, now my adventure can begin.

Winter rains had badly eroded the dirt road, causing the van to jerk and lunge wildly as our wheels dipped into one pothole after another.

"Look over there!" We all turned at once to see where David was pointing.

I craned my neck for a better look. "That sure looks like it could be the prison. Take the next road away from the canal, and let's see if we can get over there."

We finally pulled up in front of the facility in a cloud of dust. A fifteen-foot chain link fence supported a six-foot roll of barbed wire, all of which enclosed the five-acre prison compound. Almost all the area inside the fence was bare, dusty ground; only a trace of foliage struggled here and there. A few benches stood off to one side and a long, low U-shaped building occupied another area. So this was the boys' prison. I just stood there staring through the fence while the team got their things out of the van. The building blended with the dirt, and the dirt blended with the atmosphere. This facility wasn't adequate for two hundred and fifty chickens or goats, let alone boys.

Louie's hand touched my shoulder, "What's wrong, Carolyn? What's bothering you?"

My fingers hurt when I pulled them away from the wire fence. "I guess I'm really mad, Louie. This is absolutely disgusting, and we haven't even been inside or seen the boys yet."

The chaplain accompanied the guards as we walked toward the building and explained to the team, "This isn't a juvenile hall like you have in the United States, *it is a prison.* And in here the offenses range from minor theft to murder."

Barbara and I looked at each other, then at the chaplain. "All in here together?" we asked, almost in unison.

"The state only has one boys' facility like this," the chaplain explained. "Every delinquent boy in the state is placed in this prison."

"Terrific," I muttered. "Just one big happy family."

We rounded the corner of the building and encountered a group of scuffling young boys. The dust settled and the boys ran off, leaving a moldy taco shell. Could this garbage have been what they were fighting over?

The chaplain read my thoughts. "Not much is thrown away around here. Any crumb is a real treasure."

The U-shape of the prison building surrounded a dilapidated basketball court. Five or six boys halfheartedly played a scrimmage game of basketball. Most of the older boys crouched listlessly against the building. Just as at the men's prison, arms reached out from between the bars in the windows.

David's natural ease with the Spanish language gave him a freedom in this work that I envied. I sat down on a splintery old bench to watch his lively conversation with the chaplain and a prison guard. The staccato of their foreign words left me clueless. As I looked around at this absolutely barren place I remembered the words I had spoken to my staff only the night before. I had everything I wanted, but there was something missing. These boys had nothing. Everything was missing. I was restless with plenty, but they had ceased their restlessness and wallowed in despair or apathy.

David nudged me over and sat down. "We'll have to wait a few minutes before we do anything with the boys. Apparently the guard, Senor Manuel, feels powerful today, and we're the audience he needs to demonstrate his greatness."

Senor Manuel was a big man who didn't really pick up his feet as he walked, he just sort of moved along. An unkempt mustache covered his lips, and his dark, greasy hair looked as though he may have combed it once—a long time ago. His uniform was so small that the sleeves strangled his fat, pimpled arms. I looked for the expression in his eyes, but there wasn't any.

Senor Manuel fiercely rang the bell that hung on the prison wall. As the sound vibrated down his arm and into his body, he was transformed into a powerful military general.

Pandemonium broke loose. From everywhere, boys raced to the center of the basketball court. They scurried to find their exact places in line, quickly measuring an arm's length between themselves. The smaller boys formed the first row and so on until the biggest finished up the last of ten equal rows.

I couldn't believe it. Two hundred fifty filthy, mostly barefoot soldier boys—not fighting for liberty or freedom, but for survival.

The military formation jelled a split second before one of

the older boys flew into position. This was Senor Manuel's cue. His clenched teeth rippled his cheek muscles as fiery hatred smoldered in his eyes. His several chins quivered with determination. With quick, jerky steps he moved between the rows, grabbed the young boy by the shoulder and neck, and shoved him to the ground. He drew a billy club from his belt.

The stage was set and Senor Manuel was ready. We stood helplessly, forced to hear the sickening thuds of his club as it struck the boy's head and back. The boy tried desperately to protect himself, but it was no use.

Barbara was seething! "You snake," she hissed. John quickly hushed her, fearful that any sign of opposition might land us, like the redheaded American, in prison.

Satisfied with his awesome justice, Senor Manuel pushed the beaten boy toward his place in the formation. All the boys stared straight ahead, the sweat of terror running down their faces. They hardly seemed to breathe.

How cruel, how desperately cruel! I couldn't bear to think that a boy may have been beaten so that this Senor Manuel could impress the visitors with his control. As I looked at the boy, I saw tears streaming down his face, but he didn't make a sound.

Bells and regimented marching continued for some time, but at last our whole team was allowed to be alone with the boys in their prison dorm. The double steel doors slammed behind us, the echo reverberating through the room. I felt like a prisoner myself. General guards patrolled outside, looking in occasionally through the barred windows.

The first thing I noticed about the dorm was the damp, filthy dirt floor beneath my feet. Counting bunks, I slowly realized that all two hundred fifty boys shared the same room. The steel-framed beds were jammed together, touching on the sides, so the boys had to crawl onto them over the ends. The walls were made of large gray stone blocks with barred windows, evenly spaced.

"Barbara, look," I said. "There's no glass in the windows. It must be freezing in the winter. I think the first cold wind would kill me off. Most of these beds don't even have mattresses or blankets." Barb pointed out that a rough cord served as springs—an occasional cot was covered with a rough burlap material.

"Carolyn!" someone called. It was David. "Look at this barrel of water. Little Jose, here, tells me they drink it." It was teaming with parasites and covered with scum. I couldn't stand to breathe the air around it, let alone drink the putrid stuff.

I had had enough. "Play, Danny; play something happy." I slumped down onto a trunk that we used to transport our puppets. If we could, we would bring some happiness to these kids.

Danny Barker is my kind of musician; when he plays, everyone sings! We had brought along a tiny electric piano and Danny began to play it. The boys immediately clamored for the closest seats. You could hardly call the damp, hard floor the loge, but the boys didn't seem to mind. They were already carried away by the magic of Danny's lively playing.

Amelia had been interpreting events for our singing group since we'd arrived. Now that they were singing, she could sit down. I motioned for her to come sit beside me. In low tones she whispered, "That beating really upset some of the team. That poor boy!"

Quickly I looked for the young victim again but couldn't find him. Instead, my eyes caught sight of one little guy, maybe eight or nine years old, on top of one of the bunks in the back corner of the room. Several older boys sat on the same bunk. As the little tyke attempted to climb down, the others pushed him back. He was determined and pushed with all of his might against the gang while they laughed at his eagerness and pushed him back up against the wall where he had started. Not letting them thwart his plan, he came right back at two older boys, who continued to taunt him. My heart jumped as one of the older boys wickedly jabbed his fist into the little one's stomach. Tears filled his eyes, and he gritted his teeth, doubled up his small fist, and started to swing wildly. Still laughing, the older boys threw their arms over their faces and heads to ward off the little tornado's attack. A few more older boys joined the fun, and they all shoved the little one off the top bunk onto the hard floor. Ugly-sounding words could be heard above the music.

Jeers from the gang of older prisoners followed this little dynamo as he clawed and fought his way over the mess of grimy bodies. He didn't stop until he'd settled his skinny body in the very front row only about four feet from Danny. My little friend, your determination intrigues me, I thought to myself. I couldn't take my eyes off him. He became enthralled with the music and singing instantly. His body relaxed, and a huge, radiant smile swept across his face. His dark eyes, so full of depth and feeling, captured my attention and my imagination. His sparkling eyes were what made him stand out from the rest. This little guy drew something from very deep within me. I could hardly believe he was doing this to me. Who was this child and how could he smile in such a hellhole as this?

Chapter Five

The music team was doing an excellent job. By this time everyone in the room was actively involved. Most of the boys were laughing, clapping, and singing along as they learned the simple choruses the team was teaching them. But outsmiling and outsinging them all was the little tiger in the front row. A glowing happiness filled his eyes as though he had been transported to some heavenly place. I had certainly never seen a kid respond to one of our programs as this one did.

I noticed a roughly carved cross on a dirty piece of string hanging from his neck and wondered if he had made it—or maybe his mother had given it to him. His eyes, I kept thinking to myself, what incredible eyes!

My concentration on the boy was broken as Barbara nudged me in the side. "Carolyn, look at the little boy in the front row, the one with the blue jacket and the cross. Look at the expression on his face, and especially in his eyes!"

"Isn't he something!" I agreed. "I've been watching him for quite a while and I just can't get over him. Why do you think he's here?" She shrugged and kept staring at him.

From behind the piano, one of the team members slipped her arm into a colorful puppet and brought him to life. As he came before her audience, there was a gasp of excitement. The boys sat absolutely still as the puppet preacher took on his own personality and began telling them a story about Jesus. Their young eyes were glued to the puppet. We couldn't have asked for more. I thought of the wealth and abundance that we had come from in the United States, but realized I'd never had a richer experience than this moment—what a great reward.

Danny slipped off the piano stool, crouched low, and moved toward us, careful not to distract the boys. Danny was obviously enjoying all of this. His eyes sparkled as he spoke:

"Carolyn, look at the little guy in the front row with the big smile."

Barbara and I chuckled. Now Amelia, Barbara, Danny, and I all sat enthralled, watching a small boy in absolute bliss. He was so involved with the story that he didn't even notice our stares.

After a bit, I felt a tap on my shoulder and turned to hear Louie say, "Carolyn, have you noticed that little boy in the front row? His eyes are something else."

I couldn't believe it! Was there only one boy in this room, or over two hundred? Who in the world was this captivating little stranger, and what was he doing in this filthy prison? What could he possibly have done? Perhaps he had stolen some candy, or maybe bread for his family? Maybe he'd just been out on the streets and they'd caught him begging. Whatever it was, I knew with everything in me that this child did not belong here.

After more singing, David spoke to the boys about his own life and how God had come to mean so much to him. As he finished, the boys crowded around to talk to each of the team members. Because he spoke Spanish, David was popular with the boys and had to move quickly to get a word with me. "Carolyn, did you catch a look at that cute little boy in the front row? The one in the blue jacket? You should have seen his eyes!"

I had already been looking around to see where he'd gone, and while David talked, I spotted his blue jacket on the far side of the piano.

"Come on, David. Let's go over and talk to him."

Now we were beside the little fellow and discovered his eyes were every bit as expressive as we thought. We watched as he reached up to the keyboard of the piano and gently pressed down one of the keys. The piano responded with a blast of sound, and as the note came through the speakers, his eyes danced with excitement. Seeing us, he jerked himself back from the piano and covered his face. *"Hola, chico,"* David spoke tenderly and touched the boy's shoulder. He uncovered his face when he realized that we weren't going to hit him for touching the piano but hung his head, looking embarrassed.

"Como se llama?" David encouraged him to tell us his name. A frantic look came over his face, and he stared at the dirt floor. David gently repeated the question: *"Como se llama?"* The boy remained silent. Surely he knows his name, I thought. David glanced at me and motioned toward the little boy's shoulders. I could see them trembling beneath his tattered shirt. We only wanted to talk with him, not scare him to death.

Again trying to reassure him, David asked, *"Como se llama?"* Barely raising his head, he looked apprehensively at David and opened his mouth to speak.

Oh good, he was going to tell us his name. I stepped closer, not wanting to miss what he was about to say. Rather than his name, however, a series of repeated syllables and high-pitched shrieks escaped his lips. His eyes filled with tears as he dropped his head, now totally embarrassed.

"I can't make out what he's saying." David was a little unnerved. "I don't know if he's stuttering, or what! It's almost as if he's having some sort of minor convulsion." The once-radiant little face now registered stark terror. He edged away from David's arm. A simple question had shattered his momentary joy. If David was unnerved, I was crushed. His fun was over, and the reality of his grim life had become overwhelming. I had to get to the bottom of this unhappy mystery.

Earlier, one of the guards had been quite friendly and helpful as we set up our equipment. "Let's go ask the nice guard, Armando, about him. He should know his name." I led the way.

As we walked toward the barred window a strange thing happened. The little boy turned his head to watch us and then, at a safe distance, followed us. He didn't want us too close, but he didn't want us to leave, either. You rascal, I thought. He reminded me of a puppy I'd once found. We'd eventually became famous friends, but right now, a friendship with this kid seemed impossible.

David pointed the boy out to Armando and asked if he knew anything about him. With controlled affection the guard winked at the boy and said, "Yes, that's Antonio. Antonio Hernandez Sanchez. His mother didn't want him, so she just dumped him off here at La Granja. He's been living here since he was about five."

I stared at the guard in disbelief. "What do you mean, 'she didn't want him'? In the first place, who wouldn't want this darling little Antonio? And since when do people just drop their kids off at the local penitentiary—in any country!" Angry questions shot out of my mouth in rapid fire. "Are there other boys in this prison for the same reason?"

David interpreted. "No, senorita, most of them are very bad." Armando seemed very sure of himself on this point.

"How could something like this happen? And what will become of an innocent five-year-old boy left at the mercy of the prison system?" I directed questions in English at David, expecting him to repeat them to the guard. But David knew that I was getting frustrated and that the guard didn't have the answers anyway.

I thought of Antonio's mother. She'd not only rejected him, she'd had to hate him to leave him here in this cesspool. I could just imagine life in this place: deprived of love, beaten, starved, intellectually undeveloped, spiritually denied, and probably sexually molested—the list of injustices went to infinity.

Wisely assessing the situation, David came to the guard's rescue. "Let's go talk to Antonio some more."

"Just a minute, David! If Antonio's only in here because his mother didn't want him, there has to be something we can do to help him—to at least try to get him out of this prison. We'll find someone who does want him. Let's go find Amelia and ask her if she can help find a home for him. David, I think that we can get him out of this smelly hole."

By this time we were used to hearing random notes from the piano echo through the dorm. But I turned to see who'd curiously pressed down a key this time. It was young little Jose, the youngster who had so eagerly shown us the stagnant drinking water. While he was still enjoying his brief performance, Senor Manuel appeared. To prove a point, Senor Manuel suddenly reeled around and smashed the back of his hand into Jose's mouth. Blood gushed from several places as the terrified little one shrank back to take refuge on his rickety bunk.

Amid the commotion, I tried to tell Amelia about Antonio. She suggested that we attempt to visit the Office of Juvenile Records for complete details on Antonio's abandonment.

We certainly would. Nothing could keep me away! I just hoped his mother wasn't around—for fear of what I might do if she were.

That terrifying bell was ringing again. We immediately backed ourselves into a corner to stay out of the boys' way. They scrambled wildly to find their positions in front of their beds, and I quickly prayed that no one would be late.

Senor Manuel seemed to appreciate the sound of his own voice and became more theatrical with each word. We were his captive audience once again. All the boys stood at rigid attention before their bunks, absolutely silent. Senor Manuel drew a deep breath, allowing his chest to visibly rise, and began to strut down the middle of the dorm. The careless handling of his billy club terrified the boys. Many of them obviously had been recent victims of his cruelty and flinched nervously as he passed. This cocky jerk was really beginning to bug me. "David, what is he saying now?"

"The boys have to work for a while right after lunch, and he's telling them what they have to do. He is also threatening them about what he'll do to them if they don't work well. I don't think you want me to translate what he's saying." David never took his eyes off Senor Manuel while he raged at the boys. Disgust and anger were reflected in David's face; I knew how he felt.

Senor Manuel concluded his dramatic speech and proceeded to ring the prison bell. Instantly the boys responded, scattering in all directions to begin their work.

"Uh, oh, here he comes," David said. David stepped forward and talked with him briefly, then Senor Manuel left the dorm. "Guess what! He said that we could spend some more time with the boys if we want to wait until they finish their work. He must like what we're doing. I guess it keeps the boys entertained for him."

I made some quick calculations and said, "Listen, everyone. Louie, why don't you, Danny, Barb, and John organize the team and help the kids with their work. David, Amelia, and I are going back into town to the Office of Juvenile Records to find out more about this Antonio." Thumbs up, the team demonstrated their approval.

Before we could get out the steel-barred door, a commotion at the end of the dorm distracted me, and I decided to investigate. Just in front of the wall at the end of the dorm was a six-foot cement partition, open at both ends. Behind the partition was a urinal and something resembling a toilet, with a badly broken seat. Generous, I thought, considering that this dorm housed over two hundred boys.

Several little boys had rusty, dented buckets filled with some kind of foul-smelling disinfectant that they were throwing against the walls. As the liquid hit the wall it created a green slime that oozed downward. They frantically tried to catch it with mops and smear it around the toilet and urinal. None of them had on any shoes, and green slime ran down their legs and over their feet. The sight of all this was nauseating, and the smell was unbearable. As I headed for the door, I called out to Louie, "Have fun, you guys! And see if you can find out any more about our mystery boy."

"Right, we'll do that. Good luck, Carolyn!"

Chapter Six

The ride from the boys' prison revived my body and spirit. I was careful not to dwell on the many things that troubled me. The ugliness of the prisons had been so intense that I tried to let go of it and think of something else for a few minutes, but it was impossible. David and Amelia seemed to be lost in their own thoughts, too. Ordinarily, the beautiful green farmland would have been a distraction, but not this time. Fortunately we knew the way this time. So much had happened already today that it seemed like years since we'd had breakfast back at our camp.

We entered a dingy-looking building marked Office of Juvenile Records in a narrow alley on the outskirts of town, not far from the men's prison. I thanked God that Amelia had not only known enough to send us here but had known where to find the office.

Inside, the room was crowded with five desks, and lined up before each one were several families and their many children. I only breathed when absolutely necessary. The air was smelly, hot, and stagnant. It would feel so great to wash my hands and face. At least two babies cried continually, and one older man coughed so terribly that I imagined the air thick with tuberculosis germs. All these people were waiting to check their records, sign documents, or set court dates. No one looked especially happy.

While we waited in line, I thought about little Antonio and imagined some rather clever solutions. Maybe they'd be glad to get rid of him and suggest that Amelia take him home right away. I was sure we could find a loving home for him without any trouble.

At last, we walked up to the first desk. "Hi, my name is Carolyn Koons." David interpreted each phrase. "I'm a university professor doing some work here in Mexico. This is David Johnson, my assistant, and Amelia Rattan, a missionary here in the valley." I gave this lengthy introduction in hopes that our credentials would get us what we wanted. "We have just returned from La Granja boys' prison and would like to see the records of a little boy named Antonio Hernandez Sanchez."

"Oh *si,* Antonio! What a tragedy." She responded to his name without the slightest hesitation.

The three of us looked at each other questioningly. Why would Antonio stand out in her mind when she handled literally thousands of cases? What did she mean "tragedy"?

From filing cabinets that covered an entire wall, the secretary efficiently obtained Antonio's well-worn file. A picture fell from the folder as she opened it at her desk. For a sober moment I looked into the saddest eyes I had ever seen. David and Amelia were close at hand, hanging over my shoulder to get a good look at the picture. I talked to the secretary as if she understood English. "Yes, this is the boy we found at La Granja. I just can't understand why his mother didn't want him and why the authorities let her dump him off in the prison."

The secretary looked to David for the translation. "Oh no, senorita!" The secretary continued, shaking her head no, and I knew that we were about to hear the truth about Antonio—finally. Looking me squarely in the eyes, she said, "Antonio Hernandez Sanchez is in prison for *murder.* He's been there since he was five years old!"

Surely I'd just misunderstood what she said, but Amelia confirmed the horror. "He's been in prison since he was five years old, for murder! Whom does a five-year-old murder?"

The secretary went on, "They say that Antonio murdered his baby brother."

I felt sick and numbly lowered myself onto a chair. Vaguely, I recall David and Amelia sitting beside me. My head was spinning from the words of the secretary. I couldn't believe that a five-year-old could murder anyone, let alone his own brother. Somewhere something was wrong. I had seen Antonio and sensed his spirit; he wasn't a murderer. What kind of idiot would believe this stupid story? First I was shocked, then angry; I wanted to yell, "Would someone please explain this mess to me?"

The secretary squirmed in her chair, adjusted her glasses, and lifted some documents in front of her face. I guess she was trying to escape the accusing stares of the three silent, stunned Americans sitting before her.

From these documents she began to relate facts about Antonio and his case. "At 2:00 A.M., the Tijuana police were notified to investigate the death of a baby boy in one of the shacks on the outskirts of Tijuana. When they arrived, the mother and a man she was living with led them to the back of the flimsy little house. On the floor lay the broken body of a lifeless infant. A bloody wooden bat lay nearby. 'Antonio did it! Antonio did it! He killed his brother! He killed his baby brother.' His mother shrieked the terrible accusation over and over, pointing a finger at the lifeless body. Then she began to tell how Antonio had a terrible temper and was always fighting with the kids in the neighborhood and beating up on his brothers and sisters. The baby had been crying all day and finally Antonio had frantically picked up his bat and hit his brother to make him stop crying. 'He hit the baby with the bat,' the mother's crazed voice accused.

"The police found Antonio at a neighbor's house, now deeply in shock, and took him down to the Tijuana police station. They told the mother to come the next morning at 8:00 A.M. when the office opened so that she could formally press murder charges against her own son.

"Little Antonio was taken to the men's jail and was locked up in one of the cells. By noon the next day, when his mother didn't show up, the police went back out to the little shack and discovered that the mother had spent the early hours of the morning packing up all of her meager belongings; she and the man and the other three children had disappeared. It was at that point that the police realized that she was most likely the guilty one—or possibly the man—and had accused her own son only to divert the police."

We were stunned as we heard the story. "What happened to his mother?" I asked the secretary.

"We don't know. According to our records, they sent out federal police and checked every place she'd ever lived, asked all her neighbors, and even went back to Guadalajara, where she'd once lived, to look for her. She's never been heard of since the night of the murder."

"So what did they do with Antonio? Why is he at La Granja?"

"Well, they couldn't find any of Antonio's relatives—he didn't know where they lived, either—and so the legal system just decided to keep him in the Tijuana jail. He lived in the men's prison for about a year, and right after that they transferred him over to La Granja boys' prison here in Mexicali. He has been in La Granja for close to four years."

"Four years! You mean that he's been in prison for almost all his life?"

"Yes, that's why it is such a tragedy."

My mind started whirling with hundreds of questions. "Why did they keep him in the prison if they thought that the mother had done it?"

The secretary looked at me and said, "Somebody had to take care of him."

"Then why didn't they put him in an orphanage?" I could tell that the questions were beginning to make the secretary uncomfortable. I knew I was going to have to check elsewhere if I wanted more information.

Then the secretary looked at me, pleadingly. "This is a terrible thing that has happened to Antonio. Somebody needs to get that little boy out of prison."

David, Amelia, and I walked out of the Office of Juvenile Records dumbfounded. I don't think we talked to each other at all as we drove back to the boys' prison. We were too emotionally drained. My mind whirled with questions. Tragedy? I don't understand this. I can't believe this has happened.

How could the police take a five-year-old to a men's prison in the first place? The child must have been horrified to be locked in that filthy place with all of those men. My thoughts flashed back to our brief experience at the Mexicali men's prison earlier that very day. Why didn't the police take the mother down to the police station right then? How could they believe such an unreal story? Anyway, who was that man with her? How does he fit into all of this?"

As the thoughts raced through my mind, I kept seeing little Antonio sitting in the front row of our service just a couple of hours earlier with that unmistakable twinkle in his eyes. The officials surely knew that Antonio hadn't murdered anyone. I was enraged at the injustice done to Antonio and shocked at my desire for vengeance on those who made decisions around here.

When we arrived back at La Granja, everyone was outside again. Louie spotted us coming through the gate and made his way in our direction.

"I see Senor Manuel must have been pleased with your work."

"I don't know if he was or not," Louie said derisively. Apparently something or someone is occupying his attention this afternoon, so our friend Armando is in charge."

Great! I was afraid to think what might have happened while we were away, but this was perfect.

There was a thunderous basketball game going in the center of the courtyard. The fierce competition between the American and the young Mexican team especially attracted the older boys. The younger boys sat in the shade of the building making some little craft items: crosses to hang around their necks and little pictures to hang over their beds. Every team member had five or six little boys hanging onto his body soaking up affection and asking for more.

As I took in the transformation that had taken place at La Granja in just a few hours a thrill ran up my spine. Laughter and happy screams bounced off the adobe buildings and lifted the oppression of the morning. I wondered if one bright day would count for anything? But it was a relief to see the boys actively involved in something that was good for them. Next time maybe we'll bring them some treat to eat, maybe books to read—several of the high school church groups brought down boxes of clothing. We'll need to bring some over here to the boys' prison.

A couple of team members came running over toward me, followed by a shadow of little admirers. "What did you find out? What did they say down there?" The team was really eager to hear our report. How could I tell them that Antonio was in prison for a murder that everyone knew he didn't commit? It would destroy the happy atmosphere.

I just asked Danny, "Will you please go get little Antonio? We want to talk with him for a few minutes first!"

"Sure, Carolyn. By the way, we did our homework and found out quite a bit about Antonio. Right now, he's in the woodshop showing the guard, Armando, the new cross that he made today. It seems that Armando is very good to Antonio. I think he really likes him. Armando is actually kind of a teacher here, a woodshop teacher. All the boys like him." Danny looked very pleased with himself. "You're really going to like this part; Armando takes Antonio to his own home sometimes on the weekends. He has other children, and they are a kind of family for Antonio."

Danny hurried off to get the boy. There was no way he could know how glad I was for Armando's interest in Antonio. It was great to know that at least someone cared for him.

I looked up to see Danny heading our way with Antonio in tow, but something was wrong. It was as if by radar all the boys knew that something was going on. Suddenly, Danny and Antonio were encircled by an angry mob of screaming boys. They viciously grabbed at Antonio, trying to take him away from Danny. Then the strangest thing happened. They started yelling—in English—"You don't want him! You don't want him! He's a murderer! He killed his brother!" The flip side of fun sang out its wicked chorus. "He's a murderer! He's a murderer! He killed his brother!" Then I saw Antonio's face and sensed his panic as he cowered against Danny. Tears began to fall down his cheeks. I charged through the angry mass of boys and grabbed Antonio myself.

"Get these kids out of here," I yelled to the team members. David took Antonio's other arm, and we all but carried him away from the boiling riot. It made me sick to think of the cruelty and suffering in Antonio's life. What seemed like a nightmare to me was real life for Antonio.

We walked to the far end of the compound and sat down on one of the splintery benches provided for visiting parents. Amelia and I sat on either side of Antonio, and David sat on the ground in front of him. David tried to reassure Antonio with a comforting hand on his knee. First I noticed that his hands were shaking, then I realized that his entire body was trembling. Poor thing, he worked frantically to wipe away his embarrassing tears, and eventually he did regain control. It was all I could do to keep my hands off his scarred little body. My arms ached to hold and comfort him, and my heart went out to his despair. It wasn't long before compassionate David was able to get Antonio to tell us his name. As he slowly raised his head, I sensed that maybe now Antonio was beginning to believe that we cared for him.

We must have sat there for a long time cherishing our newfound togetherness. A momentary peace surrounded us, and we gladly shut out the world. Searching looks passed between Antonio and us, and endless unspoken thoughts were exchanged; but we couldn't get Antonio to say any more. When he finally leaned against me and I put my arm around him, it felt so good! I was glad that I could give him a little of the love and affection he needed so much. Periodically his body would tremble again, and fresh tears would fall. I wanted to just grab him and walk him right out through that gate only a hundred feet away. If I could just get him out of this place! He was so awfully helpless, and there was so little we could do to help him. We all cried plenty that day within the intimacy of our little circle.

The late afternoon breeze was refreshing after the exhausting heat of the day. I knew that we had to be going soon; I couldn't expect Forrest to keep dinner waiting indefinitely. I felt drained and not especially hungry, but I knew my team was starved.

I was just wondering how to tell Antonio we had to go when I saw Armando coming across the field. First, he smiled warmly at Antonio, as if to say, "Hang in there, you'll make it." Then, he looked at me. "This boy doesn't belong here. Please, do something to get him out!"

This was really getting tough. I knew lots of people would make a home for a darling little boy, but when it came to sharing your home with a murderer . . .

David explained to Antonio that we had to leave but would try to come again soon. A painful look of disappointment swept across his face, and he looked down—not wanting us to catch him showing his feelings.

It was so hard to leave. I glanced back as we passed through the gate to freedom. Antonio stood there by himself, quietly watching us.

I knew that Armando was right; Antonio didn't belong here. But, dear God, what could I do?

Chapter Seven

I was lost in thought, trying to imagine what could possibly correct the injustice we had witnessed today, when I realized we were back in Cuernavaca, home village.

The van rolled neatly into its reserved parking place and shimmied to a stop. "Thanks, ol' thing," I said and patted its very dusty dashboard. It had been a long day and I was glad to be back at camp.

Before getting out of the van, I turned and looked at my team. They were tired and hungry, but all were keenly aware that they'd been part of a very special day. "You can be proud of yourselves today. We were in several difficult situations and you all used your heads. Thanks for being there!" I smiled at them.

As I slipped to the ground from my high seat, the unmistakable aroma of turkey and dressing awakened my appetite; dinner sounded good after all. Hordes of students and staff were perched around eating. "Let's go eat, if there's anything left." The serving area of our kitchen was a giant army tent where long tables held mountainous containers of food. Everyone passed down the serving tables, then went outside to eat. To avoid the long line, Barb and I slipped up behind the servers with our empty plates, just as Forrest came through the kitchen door with a tray of turkey.

"Caught ya red-handed," he said. "Starving people do drastic things. Did you learn those bad manners at the prison?"

The thought of manners in the prison made me laugh. "We learned a lot of survival tactics today, but none of them were this easy."

Barb never let me down. "Yeah, Forrest, down there they

stab the cook before they steal the food."

"Funny, Barb! But I understand you've had quite a day. What's this I hear about a five-year-old who killed a baby? Is it true?"

"No, it's not true! Our only problem is convincing everybody else it's not true!" I responded.

"Hey, hey!" Ron was at my elbow. "Rough day, huh?"

"Rough, but challenging! Do we have an incredible story to tell you guys!"

I hated for anyone to think badly of Antonio. He wasn't just a kid in prison anymore. He had become our friend! So as we ate I began telling Ron and Forrest about our day. As I neared the end of my story, David approached and quickly realized what was happening. "Carolyn, you can't imagine how many times I've repeated this story already. The entire camp is talking about Antonio."

Ron, Forrest, and I had been sitting on the tailgate of a truck to eat our dinner, so when David joined us we moved up into the bed of the truck for more space.

"That's truly a remarkable story, Carolyn. Was it hard to leave him this afternoon?" Ron well knew that he was asking a loaded question.

"I couldn't believe it. It was so hard to walk away from him —just leave him there. You've got to see this boy, Ron! He's so appealing and so helpless."

Ron chuckled, "That sounds like something my wife would say!"

David shot up from his seat on the truck, breaking his plastic fork in his enthusiasm. "I have an idea. Instead of our staff meeting right now, why don't we set up the P.A. system and tell everyone about what happened today?" Before I could give my consent, he was gone. Little puffs of dust exploded around his feet as he jumped from the truck and ran toward the staff room. Seconds later, he was coming out with a microphone box and cord.

Groups of students and staff still ate; others were preparing for evening meetings in the villages. But when David turned up the volume on the P.A. system and announced a special group meeting, everyone assembled eagerly, taking their places on planks of wood placed neatly on the ground in the shape of an amphitheater. Everyone sat exactly two inches off the ground, but it was enough to keep them out of the dirt.

I made my way toward our makeshift platform, part of the paraphernalia that we haul down to our rustic camp every year. David had already started the group out with a song, and five hundred voices carried very well in the dimming daylight. As we sang I prayed earnestly for God's power in my life; this day had become one of the most unusual and emotionally exhausting days I had ever experienced. I wanted everyone there on the ground surrounding me to experience what we all had that day. I stood there at the mike looking at the staff and students—five hundred strong. What a wealth of God's power they possessed! I was surprised to find myself becoming nervous as I started to speak. Maybe I was just tired, or maybe I'd been more moved by this whole experience than I realized.

A hush fell over the camp as I retold our amazing story. The young people hung on my every word, and Antonio's plight became indelibly etched in their hearts.

Once again I looked deeply into the faces before me. "We need to pray this boy out of prison. He doesn't belong there. Let's ask God to get him out. I believe he will!" Before I could get the last word out, applause broke out throughout the camp. I was too moved to say any more. As I walked over to the side of the stage and sat down, Ron quickly went up and asked the group to make a commitment to pray for Antonio until we got him out. We were going to start right now.

As we prayed I could hear Armando saying, "Get him out of here, he doesn't belong here."

As young person after young person stood up to pray, I sensed the spirit of God moving within our camp. A calm came over my spirit; I felt God's presence and direction. I'd been praying for years, and I knew God heard my voice, but this experience was different, somehow—more specific. "Get Antonio out of prison," God told me. "Take one step at a time, and don't take no for an answer." As I joined in the concluding hymn, I was absolutely sure that this was God's plan, not mine. To think that just yesterday I had told God that I was ready for whatever he wanted me to do. He certainly didn't waste any time!

Apparently he'd worked out some of the details as well. My good friend Happy, looking unusually worthy of her name, sat down beside me. "Carolyn, if you can get Antonio out of prison, there's a good possibility Jerry and I could adopt him. We'd certainly like to try."

"And I'd certainly *like* you to try!" I laughed in amazement and threw my arms around her. What perfect parents they'd be for Antonio! Both Happy and Jerry were mature, in their late thirties, and they loved children. Happy had spent several years in Mexico as a missionary; she knew the language and people well. And Jerry had a special gift for dealing with troubled young people, having worked for several years in various juvenile facilities. It did occur to me that a nine-year-old might intrude on their honeymoon—they were only just married—but such details could be worked out later. What an answer to prayer. God was working fast—just my style!

During the next few days there was an air of excitement around our camp. Antonio's plight was awful, but the thought of getting him out was exhilarating. You could sense it in the air.

Our week in the Mexicali valley passed quickly. Tomorrow we would break camp, and by Sunday nearly all would be home in their own churches for Easter Sunday. One thing I knew: the young people who had come to this year's Mexicali Outreach would go back changed. Sure, they would have new spring clothes, a fresh haircut, or a bouncy new hairdo. They would attend a well-planned Easter service and enjoy their family around a fancy dinner table. But they would be different, and friends and family around them would notice. And that went for me, too.

We were just entering the city of Mexicali en route to the prison. David and his girl friend, Sue, accompanied me.

"David, do you remember Antonio's shoes?"

"Do you mean the torn canvas without shoestrings that he has around his feet?" David laughed. "Yes, I remember his tennies. I'm amazed that he can keep the filthy things on his feet."

"Why don't we stop here in Mexicali and buy him some new ones?"

David responded by pulling the van into a parking place. We piled out, feeling energized by our mission.

"To be honest, David, I don't know if this is to make Antonio feel better, or me. Tomorrow we're going home, and I'm so afraid he'll feel deserted. I wonder how many people have walked in and out of his life? Maybe the tennies will help him remember us."

We easily found the right shoes and headed toward the van. I was hugging the shoebox, deep in thought, when I almost crashed into an outdoor jewelry display. A man of rather striking appearance sat behind the counter artistically engraving names on bracelets. Sue and David had continued up the street, so I yelled after them, "Hey, wait a minute! Why don't we get him one of these bracelets? Look, we'll have his name engraved on it." I was already placing my order by the time they reached me. "While I finish here why don't the both of you run across the street and get some paper and ribbon and we'll meet at the van?"

The rutted dirt road had become familiar territory by this time, and I had become accustomed to the dust and bumps. Tenderly I examined each gift again, then carefully wrapped them with colorful ribbon and paper. I wondered if Antonio had ever seen curled ribbon.

Today was slightly cooler, and many of the boys were milling around in the prison's courtyard. Both David and I tried to conceal the gifts from the inquisitive stares of the other boys.

From across the courtyard, Antonio saw us coming and ran to meet us as fast as his legs would carry him. All of us were grinning from ear to ear as we greeted each other once again. See, Antonio, we did come back, I thought to myself.

"I feel like we're on national TV. David, where can we go to be alone with Antonio?"

David shrugged. "Beats me, Carolyn." He looked around. "We don't have many choices."

One of the splintery benches, near a poor excuse of a tree, was our only option. "Oh, for a little privacy," I sighed, but we led Antonio through the crowded courtyard to the visitors' bench. Turning our backs to the prison and the other boys, we faced the field and encircled Antonio, creating privacy of a sort.

David took the larger box from beneath his arm and put it on Antonio's lap. The delight on his young face thrilled my heart; I was so glad we had taken the time to get him something. No one spoke for fear of spoiling the moment. I felt that I hadn't experienced this much tenderness in my entire life; my emotions were going wild. Totally involved, I watched Antonio's little brown hands tenderly caress the box and ribbon. When he began to unwrap it, it was with meticulous care. His ways seemed too refined, considering his circumstances.

First, he wound up the ribbon and tucked it deep down into his pocket; then he folded the paper into a tight square and put it in his pocket, too. I remembered the chaplain saying that the moldy taco shell was a treasure. What must this paper and ribbon mean to him? At last, the lid was off and the brand-spanking-new black-and-white tennis shoes were unveiled. Too bad only a few of us were able to witness that scene. Tears of joy streaked his dirty face as Antonio pulled the shoes from the box.

I leaned down and carefully flipped his tattered shoes from his feet. "Oh, you poor kid!" I laughed. "Look you guys, he doesn't have any toes." His feet were totally caked with mud, to the point we couldn't tell where the toes ended and the mud began. I took it for granted that there must be ten little toes hidden somewhere under all that dirt. But without hesitation Antonio grinned and started to put his filthy foot into his new tennis shoes.

David thwarted the little tiger's plans, picked him up, and

laughed as he carried Antonio to a nearby hose. "Nobody's feet could be this dirty." He sat him down, rolled up his pant legs, and began washing one foot, then the other. I was sure that I'd never seen a movie this good. Antonio stood teetering over David with his arm wrapped around David's back. His face brightened with a possessive grin, and his chin went up just slightly as he enjoyed the attention of his new friend. Sue and I looked on amazed at the power of simple friendship.

With ease, David picked up his skinny little friend and carried him back over to our bench. We all watched as he carefully slipped his feet, now including ten wiggly toes, into his brand-new tennis shoes. Antonio stood up but kept looking down at his feet. He just couldn't believe that the tennis shoes were his.

The first gift had gone over so well that I decided it was time for another and took the tiny bracelet box from my pocket. When Antonio saw the box he looked at me and pointed at himself, as if to say, "For me?"

"*Si,* for you," I gestured, and handed it to him. Just as carefully as the first, he unwrapped the gift and tucked the wrappings away in his pocket.

His mouth fell open, and his big brown eyes bulged out in surprise when he saw the tiny silver bracelet lying there. He didn't even try to speak this time. When he didn't move to take it out of the box, I helped him and put it on his arm.

David spoke to him and explained that his name was written on the bracelet. Antonio rubbed his finger over the letters as if he were reading braille, "Ah-Ah-An-ton-i-o." His own name finally came out of his mouth. He had finally spoken! As he looked up, tears began to fill his eyes, and we all laughed and hugged.

Our time was rapidly slipping away, and I pulled my tiny calculator watch from my pocket to check the time. The unusual little instrument caught Antonio's attention. He'd never seen such a strange thing. He was so attracted to it that he kept staring at my pocket after I put it away.

Sue asked if she could see it for a minute. Before we knew

what was happening, we were all enjoying a brief math lesson between her and Antonio.

"His education must be very basic," offered David. "Armando said that a volunteer teacher comes once a week for a few hours, but that the class isn't mandatory."

I took a pen and some paper from my notebook and asked Antonio if he could write his name. He looked at me, then at David and Sue, and then back at me. We'd forgotten the need to translate! When David repeated the question in Spanish, Antonio beamed. Apparently the answer was yes. He labored over each letter as though carving them in stone. When it was all down—David having surreptitiously added the final *0,* Antonio held up his bracelet for comparison. Now we knew for sure that he understood what was written on the bracelet.

As if sensing the late hour, Antonio hesitantly took the calculator watch from Susan and put it in my hand. I wrapped my fingers around it tightly, desperately fighting the urge to give it to him. This separation might be a long one, and my concern for Antonio went deeper than his need for material comforts or friends. "David," I asked haltingly, "Please tell him about God. Tell him that he's not alone!"

"Antonio, do you believe in God?" he asked.

Immediately he reached for the cross that hung around his neck and grinned proudly at us as he held it out. So David went on to explain that five hundred young people, just like himself, were praying for a miracle in his life. "We're asking God to be real good to you, and he will because he loves you."

We didn't go any further because we didn't want to make his stay in prison any more difficult. When I was more certain about what would be happening, I would tell him. For now he seemed comforted and put his hand on David's shoulder, as if to say he understood everything.

I compromised my urge to give him the calculator. I reached for his hand and put it on top of the calculator and said, "Some day I would like you to visit me in the United States, and maybe when you come you will get a calculator, too!" As David's interpretation settled into Antonio's mind, his smile spread to his eyes; he threw his arms around my waist, and we all shared a teary-eyed hug.

Each of us pulled papers from our wallets and quickly wrote our names and addresses on the back. I very carefully wrote my home phone number on the back of mine and handed it to Antonio. David handed the other papers to Antonio and sternly instructed, "Never lose these. If you need help, call us. We'll write to you; Armando can help you read our letters. We'll come back as soon as we possibly can." Little did we know that these precious treasures—the bracelet and the security of the phone numbers—would last no more than one day; a gang of older boys plundered the scant possessions of the young one while he slept.

I hated the awful fence that stood between us. Antonio leaned against it as we got into our car, then waved as we drove away. I wonder if he thought we would ever return.

Chapter Eight

Stately oak trees shade the manicured lawns and shrubs lining the street I live on and lend a peaceful sense of permanence and tranquility. An interesting contradiction within me surfaces each time I return home. A rugged individual leaves home, begging to be challenged and offering unlimited commitment to whatever each day brings. But full-throttle living skids into a craving for convenience and comfort as I turn homeward. Images of my own comfortable waterbed, my cozy breakfast nook, and a long, hot shower quicken my pace, and I can hardly wait to get unpacked.

This early spring day was nearly perfect, with temperatures in the mid-seventies and a light breeze holding the smog at bay. Everything was a luscious green from the exceptionally heavy winter rains. This was Southern California at its best; in my opinion an ideal place to live.

Traveling is a way of life with me; frequent trips decorate my calendar with excitement. My travels reunite me with old friends and thrill me with new ones, so I rarely turn down an invitation for a conference or a speaking engagement. Unequivocally, I am a people lover and adventure seeker!

With all my going and coming, it's been necessary to perfect a pretty slick routine for packing and unpacking. Many of the basics I own in duplicate; one set stays packed permanently. After pulling into the garage, it was only minutes before my sleeping bag was in its place on the shelf, a load of dirty laundry was washing, and the rest of my things were in the house. I was re-established in my house, my cozy two-story condominium—my castle and refuge from the world. Its cupboards were filled with my kind of food, its closets lined with my favorite clothes; if I went to bed late no one cared. Most important, no one made me feel guilty about anything.

Before settling down, I ran back outside for the mail and returned with two full armloads. Coming through the door I awkwardly reached over and turned up the thermostat; the house was a bit cool.

"Hi, fish"; a sprinkle of food brought them hungrily to the surface. It was great to be home and relish the feeling of wiggling my toes into the deep brown carpet that went throughout my house. With my huge stack of mail, I plopped down in front of the TV to catch the news. The house seemed peaceful and welcoming; after sorting my mail I puttered around contentedly for about an hour.

Then the inevitable happened. The clock ticked too loudly, and my house was too quiet—maybe one of the fish had died. I recognized this restless feeling as just part of my routine after an especially exciting week. And that's just what Mexicali had been, exciting. My family of five hundred and all the hustle and bustle that accompanies that many people had cooled down to one, me. I needed to come down a bit more slowly.

I took up the phone and rang my good friends Don and Pauline Grant. As dean of the university, Don was always interested in hearing about Mexicali, both personally and professionally—they both were. They were glad to hear from me, and we arranged to meet for dinner.

Mexico had been dreadfully hot; feeling clean and pretty again seemed like an elusive dream. After a sudsy shower, I carefully applied my makeup and dried and curled my shortish hair. I chose a silky, rose-colored blouse that made me feel both rich and feminine. I added black pants, an expensive-looking dark gray crocheted sweater, and a mass of fine gold chains around my neck, and surveyed myself in the mirror. My reflection looked decidedly tall, slim, and beautiful, a perfect catch for a good-looking, intelligent, rich young bachelor—in that order. I laughed at myself and walked away from the mirror. I loved looking, feeling, and doing my best. Life was too much fun to waste on any kind of mediocrity.

A short time later, we were having dinner in a nearby

restaurant, deeply engrossed in the details of Antonio and the prison. At the story's conclusion, Don addressed me thoughtfully: "I've known you for a long time, Carolyn, but this caper is the craziest thing you have ever been involved with. If you can ever get that boy out of prison, it'll be a miracle. But if anyone can, it's you. Antonio is a lucky little kid to have you for a friend!"

Don was right, what single college professor in her right mind would get entangled with the Mexican government over a nasty murder case involving a little boy? "This whole thing sounds crazy, but I feel positively that this is what God wants me to do."

The rest of the dinner hour was very pleasant as we exchanged news and I caught up on what had happened at the university that week. Then Don asked seriously, "This year's Mexicali was one of the greatest ones yet, wasn't it, Carolyn?"

"Yes, I'm sure of it. And I feel as though this week is just the beginning of a brand-new adventure for me."

"You and your Mexicali team should share what happened down there during one of our chapel hours. Why don't I see what I can do?" Don's enthusiasm encouraged me.

"No question about it, Don. We would love the chance to tell the rest of our student body. Just let me know when, and we'll be there. I would hate to keep this incredible story a secret. Anyway, we need all the support we can get!"

I went home satisfied with the closeness we shared. Good friends are important, and the Grants were like family. Finally my restlessness was spent, and I gladly enjoyed a peaceful evening alone. My work schedule would be grueling once it got started again, so I had better take the opportunity to get some rest.

My office at the university is a fun place to be. It's a hive of activity, where optimism and possiblity are encouraged and no one is a failure until they stop trying.

In addition to teaching my Christian Education classes fulltime, I direct the Christian Service Department, several clubs and service organizations, an employment office, and of course, Mexicali Outreach. My office is home base for all these activities. We may sometimes appear chaotic, but the busier I am, the happier I am, and my office reflects my attitude.

By the time I reached my office the Monday morning after our eventful week in Mexico, it seemed as though everyone in the school was already talking about Antonio Hernandez Sanchez. Word had spread like a brush fire fanned by strong winds of interest. Every office and classroom buzzed with a version of little Antonio's plight, until everyone was keenly interested in hearing the real story in its entirety.

I entered my office with several students, and we chattered like an army of happy chipmunks. I wrote out instructions for my secretary, Sonja, and picked up my messages. Soon I was back to work and very happy.

Within two days I was with the Mexicali Outreach team in the APU chapel sharing our experience. Over a thousand lively college students held their restlessness in check and focused intently on the story we told. We concluded by praying for Antonio; I sensed a real strength and commitment as the students agreed to keep praying for him until he was released. My confidence grew; surely if all these students believed and prayed, Antonio would soon be released. Feeling really good about all this support, I wrote Antonio a letter immediately.

By the end of the week the office was running smoothly enough for me to call Amelia and ask her to put me in contact with a good Mexican lawyer—only to discover that she had already contacted Senor Dominguez, a Mexican lawyer considered excellent in his field.

Wild optimism overcame my initial fear that we would have to work with lawyers who didn't speak English. I felt at a disadvantage in Mexico because of my poor Spanish, but with Amelia and David and now a really good lawyer, we would do just fine.

Two weeks later, David and I traveled to Mexico, picked up Amelia, and went to the office of Senor Dominguez, who was head of his own law firm. The office was modern and professional-looking. We were escorted through the pleasant outer office to the boss's suite, and my hope escalated when I saw a file folder on top of Senor Dominguez's desk conspicuously labeled *Antonio Hernandez Sanchez*. Good, he already has some information compiled, I thought, a good sign.

Amelia, David, and I accepted the proffered seats in front of his desk and watched as he made himself comfortable. His brown suit and white shirt accentuated a crispness in his manner. "I have checked out all of Antonio's records," he began, and then relayed to us exactly the account we had heard from the secretary at the Juvenile Court. He continued, "I have also met with the three judges at the Juvenile Court, the director of the prison, and Antonio himself."

Everything he said evidenced competence, but his tone was too grave, and I could feel my defenses going up.

Senor Dominguez paused only briefly. "Antonio cannot be released. He is in prison for murder. And we can't find his mother, who has legal right to him for six years after her disappearance." I had questions at this point, but he went on. "The judges said that you can have almost any other boy in La Granja that you want, but not Antonio." At once, Senor Dominguez pulled out two other file folders. He had painstakingly performed his legal obligation to Antonio, turning every possible stone. His voice sounded like background music as he described two adoptable boys. My mind was back at his earlier statements, but he went on. "See, here is a little boy who has only been in for three months. He's about eight years old; isn't he handsome?"

I mockingly thought of a mother gently prying a hairpin from her screaming baby's fist, and pacifying her with a cookie. It wasn't as if I *needed* a little Mexican boy. Getting Antonio out of prison was a responsibility, and I had God to answer to. I wasn't finished—even if Senor Dominguez had closed his books on Antonio.

As I studied the lawyer's face, then looked into his eyes, I realized that he wasn't a fighter. "I came for Antonio, Senor Dominguez, no other boy."

"It is a shame, Senorita Koons, but the court said that you cannot have Antonio. No one can. He is the only boy in the system right now in for murder. Won't you consider one of these?" His gaze lingered on my face as he held out the other folders.

Defiance dripped from my single word, "No!" As I remembered my "deal" with God—"Get Antonio out and don't take no for an answer!"—my commitment deepened.

The exasperated lawyer skimmed the folders across his desk and looked at me as if to say, "You stubborn American woman!" Then he began to ask me some questions. "Why can't you take another boy? Why do you want to get mixed up in a murder case? What's so special about Antonio Sanchez?"

The answers were clear to me. "This may sound very strange to you, but we believe this boy is innocent, and we want to help him get out of prison and into a home. There are over a thousand people now praying to God for his release; you see, giving up isn't an option for me. I don't think he killed anyone, and he doesn't belong in that prison—and in my opinion, that's the crime!"

A weariness settled into Senor Dominguez's face, and he sighed deeply, "Senorita Koons, according to his records, they are going to keep him in La Granja until he is seventeen, and then they are going to release him."

I quickly figured, "But that means that he will have been in prison for twelve years of his life. They can't do that to him. It's a gross waste of a child's life! It would destroy him!"

Mr. Dominguez dropped his eyes. "I know. They have already predicted that once they release him, he won't be able to make it on the streets for more than a month or two. I'm sure that he'll end up in the men's prison and probably spend the rest of his life there. Senorita Koons, I am very sorry about Antonio, but his case is so hopeless. Surely you could learn to like another boy?"

Again, looking him straight in the eyes, I said, "No! Antonio is my *only* choice!"

He paused, realizing he was not going to be able to sway

me, "If you are certain, then let me see what else I can do."

As we walked out of the office, exchanging glances, my certainty crystallized, "I know that God wants this boy out of prison, and God will help us."

David nodded, "Senor Dominguez is really dragging his feet, making things impossible. Why is it so hard to get this kid out? Don't they care that a person's life is being ruined?"

We decided to go back over to La Granja and visit Antonio. We wanted to be careful not to spend too much time with him, but we didn't want him to think we had forgotten him, either. As we walked back into La Granja, it was very quiet. Evidently the boys were locked in the dormitory, so we stopped at the director's office. He was fairly friendly. "Oh, *si,* you can visit Antonio. Let me send a guard for him."

Armando took up the order and departed for the dorm as we stepped outside to wait. Visiting outside would be far better than under the suspicious eyes of the director. I anticipated Antonio's sparkling eyes and bright smile and couldn't wait to ask him if he had received our letters. But the minute I saw him, I knew something was wrong. Rather than bounding across the courtyard, he poked along behind Armando a few paces and looked the picture of both dejection and starvation. He was so skinny. He must be sick, I thought. But as he came closer, I could see that he had two black eyes, both of which were deeply sunken, and a hollow look replacing his happy sparkle. Nasty scabs and bruises covered his thin face, yet a brave little smile flickered dimly as he looked up at me. David instantly knelt down before him and grasped his shoulders firmly, "Antonio, what happened?"

At last he stuttered in Spanish, "I-I-I f-fell." He looked more like he'd been kicked by a bull or hit by a train; we all knew he was covering up.

Armando stepped forward—obviously he'd been listening. His big hand covered Antonio's fragile shoulder, and he was so bent on what he was saying that he unconsciously shook the boy with each word. "He didn't fall! The boys found out that some *americanos* were interested in adopting him and that he might get out of La Granja, so they have been tormenting him and beating him up. You have got to get him out of here before they kill him!" He turned and walked away before the director caught him talking too long to us.

David and Amelia and I frantically looked at each other. "This is serious." As I put my arm around little Antonio and he snuggled close, I noticed his little hand coming up, wiping his eyes and nose as though he didn't want us to notice his tears.

"Look at his new tennis shoes," David whispered. The new shoes that had brought him so much joy just two weeks ago were unrecognizable. There was writing all over them, the laces were missing, and it was apparent that someone had taken a knife to them.

Then I noticed that the engraved bracelet was missing. "Antonio, what happened to your bracelet?" By now large tears had filled his eyes, and I reached for a tissue. We never got a response to that question, but we realized that the prison gang had plenty to do with it. I wondered if he'd got his face smashed trying to protect his new possession. I knew that we'd have to find out before giving him any more gifts.

It was harder than ever to leave little Antonio, the words of the guard fresh in our minds: "Get him out of here before they kill him!" For his sake I concealed my fears for him behind a confident smile. "Antonio, we are going to win, so be brave until I see you again." A heroic attempt to smile froze on his lips.

The long, hot, five-hour drive back to Los Angeles seemed longer than ever. I was home no more than fifteen minutes before calling the Department of Immigration in Los Angeles. This process was so new to me it was difficult to know where to start. Every office sent me to another office, until at last I reached someone who could help me, a Mrs. Meyers, who worked with international adoptions.

In describing the La Granja prison to the authorities, I decided it was better to call it a juvenile facility rather than a prison. "How long has the boy been in the facility?" "Who is going to adopt him?" I was standing in for Happy and Jerry until Antonio arrived in the United States; at that point we would immediately transfer the adoption to them. They lived four hundred miles away, and the legal process would be prohibitive financially otherwise.

"Why are you trying to get him out?" "No one knows where his mother is?" Question after question, then her response, "I'm not exactly sure what to do! We've never had a case like this. I guess we'll have to do a home study on you just as though you were adopting a boy out of an American orphanage."

"That's fine with me," and it was—it was the least I could do. The decision to be Antonio's legal guardian while his adoption by Happy and Jerry was finalized didn't take much thought. It was just another logical step.

The American immigration office gave me a huge packet of papers to be filled out for a home study on me. They couldn't figure out why a single American woman, professor at a university, was spending so much time trying to get a little Mexican boy into the United States. "This kid must be pretty special," laughed Mrs. Meyers as I walked out the door.

Turning around, I winked. "He is! He's very special!"

Three hours was my generous estimate of the time needed to complete the immigration papers. Two full days and a messy desk later, they were finally finished. A comprehensive FBI interrogation couldn't have been any more thorough. They knew more about me than my own mother! List every place that you have ever lived; name five people that knew you at each of those five places; list employment; list reasons for wanting to immigrate a child into the United States; page after page after page, the questions continued. I had to submit savings and checking account information, birth certificate, and a health certificate (after having a physical).

How many natural parents would there be if they all had to qualify first? It didn't seem like a good idea to tell Happy and Jerry about this exhaustive study; they would find out soon enough.

In the meantime, the months were beginning to slip away. We were now well into summer, and as September approached, I realized that we wouldn't be able to get Antonio into the United States by the time school started. Maybe we could get him out by January and he could start school midway through the year. Another cold winter in the prison—he was so thin already, would he make it? There were phone calls back and forth to the lawyers, back and forth to American Immigration. Immigration directors visited my home and every place I had lived in the last ten years; there were more papers for Mexico, more papers for the courts, more money to the lawyer. On it went.

I hoped that our next visit to Senor Dominguez would be encouraging. By now he should know what the courts had decided concerning Antonio. When we arrived back in Mexicali I was surprised to learn that he was not there and had turned our case over to his associate, "better qualified" to deal with such an intricate case. It was like starting all over again! "Are you sure that you don't want another boy, senorita? Any other boy? How about a girl? We have lots of orphanages in Mexico." Persistently, I hammered my determination into his dense brain. My sole reason for being here was Antonio Hernandez Sanchez. It irritated me that these people kept trying to distract me with other children.

"I'm sure that there must be many nice children available, but God has burdened my heart with one innocent boy—his name is Antonio." It was hard for me to believe that they couldn't see the grave injustice of this case and that they wouldn't accept responsibility for correcting it. Now, as I explained it to them over and over again, they seemed even more unreasonable. Did they expect a little boy to defend himself?

Suddenly, I felt these people were wasting my time and money and that I'd better think of another strategy quick. If the lawyers couldn't get any further with the judges, I decided to go see them myself. "I would like to meet with the judges myself," I announced. The lawyer looked at me in amazement.

"Really!"

"Yes," I responded confidently. "I would like to talk with them myself." Little did he know how nervous—yet determined—I was underneath all this poised dialogue. The irony of the whole mess disturbed me. Someone spoke a word and an innocent five-year-old child was thrown into prison and forgotten. Why couldn't these high-ranking lawyers and judges see the injustice and get him out? Didn't anyone care? What kind of a system was this, anyway?

Several phone calls later, David, Amelia, and I walked into the Office of Juvenile Records, where we had first heard Antonio's story. It seemed like a step backward. Strangely, at the far end of this plain building was a door that led into the official judges' chambers, where all the juvenile cases were tried. The small courtroom had drab cement walls with no pictures. There was seating for maybe twenty people, an open space, then a table behind which sat three judges. It was hard to believe that Antonio's destiny would be decided in this small room.

My turquoise and beige linen dress was supposed to make me look cooler then I felt, but perspiration and anxiety threatened to ruin my act. My throat and mouth felt dry as we entered the judges' chambers, and their candid appraisal of me didn't help me relax. I wasn't sure just what the judges expected, but something held their attention for an uncomfortable moment. It was very hot and three Mexican judges were staring at me, but my business here was very important, so I maintained a disciplined confidence.

Fortunately, David Johnson was an absolutely fluent interpreter. I needed to have perfect confidence in his ability to communicate my thoughts to these officials, and I did.

The proceedings began. The judges could not believe that

I, a single woman, was interested in getting little Antonio out of prison and into the United States. "What is your occupation?" "How long have you been at Azusa Pacific University?" When I told them that I'd been at the university for over fifteen years, they were considerably interested and asked for my financial statements, letters of recommendation, letters confirming my employment, and letters from American Immigration. My compulsiveness paid huge dividends once again, for from my bulging attaché case, I was able to produce every document they required—in duplicate. They were very impressed with my efficiency, almost startled. More drawn by curiosity than compassion, the judges became involved in Antonio's case and spent several minutes carefully going over each document.

"Why do you want him out of prison?" one of the judges asked.

Politely I asked him, "Aren't prisons for criminals?"

"Yes," he agreed.

"He hasn't committed a crime, and he doesn't belong in prison."

"The records say that he has committed murder."

"Your honor, the records show that he was *suspected* of murder, but the authorities now feel that he didn't kill anyone." I felt like a defense lawyer. The heat was on, and almost as a diversion, one of the judges asked, "Do you plan to get married?"

"Why, does that make a difference?" I grinned.

"No, I was just curious. You're going to a lot of trouble to get this boy out. He must be something special."

"He is very special," I agreed. We sensed some rapport beginning to develop between the judges and myself.

The hearing was getting hot now—if anyone could help me, it was these three judges. After they conferred between themselves for a few minutes, the senior judge addressed us in an authoritative yet friendly manner. "We'll see what we can do. This is a very unusual case and it will take some work.

We will need to research all the records on this case before we can make a final decision."

"Yes, Your Honor, I understand." But even as those words were spoken, impatience seized my heart and shouted for an immediate judgment.

In a tone of dismissal, the judge concluded, "Check back with us in one month."

I smiled and nodded respectfully, "Yes, we will, and thank you for your most gracious time and help."

As David, Amelia, and I walked toward the door, one of the judges made a remark in a humorous tone, and I turned to David for a translation. "Do you want to adopt me too?" We all laughed our way through the door.

Could Antonio survive another month in La Granja? It would seem like an eternity. Anything could happen in a month. Armando's warning blared in my memory: ". . . before they kill him." But there was nothing we could do; we were at the mercy of the court. God was trying to teach me to trust him completely. I usually tried to handle things on my own and just report back to God my progress; it wasn't going to work this time. I was going to have to trust him for the next step.

Between the heat, the stress of conversing through an interpreter, and the urgency of Antonio's situation, I was now totally exhausted and dreading the long drive back to L.A.

That month seemed more like a year, but there was a lot to be done. I'm sure glad that God said to take it one step at a time. If I'd had any idea of all of the legal complications, the papers, the lines, the meetings, the offices, and the driving back and forth, I would have been convinced the task was impossible.

Chapter Nine

A look backward at the year since we'd discovered Antonio helped me realize that we were making progress toward his release. Very slowly, very carefully, the puzzle began to come together, but it was unquestionably God's timing. From time to time impatience got the best of me and I dreamed up ways to hurry the process. Maybe we should have stuffed him into the puppet box that very first day in the prison. Lots of maybes crossed my mind, but they were only fleeting temptations.

It was impossible to hurry American Immigration, Washington, D.C., or the Mexican lawyers and judges. One very long year had passed, and if it had seemed long to me, with a busy and fulfilling life to distract me, how much longer must it have seemed to Antonio!

The Mexicali Outreach teams would soon be in full swing just as they had been a year ago. Something like disappointment nagged at me; it was hard to admit that Antonio was still in prison when I had faithfully committed to God to get him out. Was I overlooking some obvious path? Hard work, worry, and lots of money, and this job was still totally God's miracle. He would have to make it happen, but the process made me feel out of control and utterly helpless. Trusting God wasn't an option, it was the only way.

La Granja had developed quite a reputation by this time, and many of our students were vying for positions on the prison team. All of us looked forward to being with the boys, especially Antonio. Occasionally this past year we had been able to see him, but several times when we arrived he was "out" on a work project of some kind. Our visits were so terribly infrequent that missing him was a real disappointment.

This year's Mexicali Outreach agenda would include much more than previous years' because I was determined to make great strides toward getting Antonio out of prison. A rewarding visit with him in the prison set my will in concrete and my feet flying to the lawyer's office. Surely there would be some answers and he would soon be released.

Upon entering the lawyer's office where I expected to meet with Senor Dominguez or his associate, a young, dark-haired, attractive Mexican woman walked briskly and directly to greet us. Her bright eyes and animated face captivated us. Without the slightest hesitation, she quickly looked us over and then, in flawless English, introduced herself: "Hello, my name is Lupe Puga."

She maintained perfect eye contact as she shook first my hand, then Amelia's, and finally David's. Lupe seemed very pleasant, with a confident smile on her face and a spark in her eyes that told us she saw life as an adventure.

"Please come into my office, we have so much to talk over this morning, and I'm eager to get started. Please sit down and let me begin by saying—you need to understand—I am not a full-time lawyer in this office. I have just finished my college degree in law and I'm an intern here."

She was sharp, but I was reluctant to give my expensive lawyer's understudy practical experience on such an urgent and complicated case. "Forgive me for asking, but where is Senor Dominquez and his associate? We had an appointment with them."

"Of course, Carolyn. I don't mean to put you off, but I need a moment to explain."

The offices seemed deserted. I wondered what was going on. My fingers drummed impatiently on my leather satchel, reflecting the frustration of a year-long stall.

"They're gone. All the lawyers are on vacation for one month, and I've been assigned to help you with Antonio's case." Lupe picked up an over-stuffed file folder and set it on her lap to accent what she said. "Carolyn, I am going to be very honest with you. Everyone said that it's impossible to get

Antonio out of prison, including the staff here. But after studying this case line by line, covering all the steps of my superiors,
then digging even further, I don't believe it. Carolyn, I believe as you do. And if you'll trust me and let me work on this
case for you, my efforts will prove us both right the day
Antonio walks out of that prison."

My first reaction was amazement. She was so confident and
determined: it was this kind of attitude that would get Antonio
out of prison. Here was my lawyer, intern or not.

She continued, "Carolyn, I have gone ahead and worked
on the case as if you had already approved me. Please, I do
want to help you. I believe that we can get Antonio out of La
Granja. Let me take this case."

There was something about Lupe that thrilled me; she had
fight, she had enough for Senor Dominguez and his associate
combined, and then some. As she talked, our spirits seemed
to mesh and generate enthusiasm. It looked like Antonio had
captured another heart.

A quick interrogation of Lupe revealed that she was in her
late twenties, had never married, and had worked in this law
office for only two months. These were hardly the qualifica-
tions to impress an anxious American client, but her attitude
handsomely overrode any inadequacies. "Okay, Lupe, I believe you. I have only one goal. Let's get this boy out of
prison!"

She boldly opened up the file folder and flashed a poised
grin. "I have already sent a doctor out to give Antonio a
physical. We needed to make sure that he's physically sound
and also try to determine his age. The doctor estimated his age
to be somewhere around ten years old, and he seems to be in
pretty good health, although somewhat undernourished and
small for his age. I also went out and talked personally to
Antonio and to the prison director. For some reason the director was reluctant to give me any information about Antonio.
However, he did say that Antonio was a real fighter, not
willing to let anything slide, and that he was continually involved in fights at the prison." She smiled wryly and shook her

head, "Whoever gets this boy must be prepared for a battle. He may be small, but every ounce of this kid has struggled to survive at all cost!"

A warm glow spread through me; it was with that same attitude that I met life myself. Maybe that's why I was so drawn to little Antonio. But Happy and Jerry would have their hands full with this one, I thought. "Lupe, that's okay, we'll take him any way we can get him. Let's just get him out!"

"Yes, we'll get him out. Just listen to this juicy discovery that explains all the mystery in this case. While digging through the records, I was surprised to find not a single mention of the trial. So I researched further and found out *there never was a trial.*"

Nothing could surprise me anymore—actually, I had rather expected to find a flimsy excuse for Antonio's imprisonment. "He wasn't tried? Why?" I questioned, trying to visualize such a trial.

"Due to the unusual circumstances of this case, a trial was probably simply overlooked. During the investigation, Antonio couldn't be placed in an orphanage, and after a year in the men's prison, they decided that the boys' prison was the most appropriate place for him to go. There seems to have been a subtle attitude that they were really doing him a favor by not turning him out on the street." David and I looked at each other in astonishment.

For a few moments we sat in absolute silence trying to digest what Lupe had told us. David anticipated my question. "If he hasn't been tried or sentenced, how can they hold him? Why can't we just take him?"

"I wish it were that easy, David. But the fact that this case hasn't been tried yet is going to be very embarrassing for someone. An oversight such as this in the legal process may be difficult to untangle. But we do have something going for us: the judges really liked you, Carolyn. In fact, they actually seemed a little charmed by your sincerity and your ability to make things happen."

This was all very flattering, but it didn't get Antonio out

of prison. "What's the next step, Lupe? It's going to take lots more than charm to get the judge to release Antonio."

Intensity swept through Lupe as she swung behind her desk and reached for her calendar. "Yes, much more than charm. I am going to court at the earliest possibility and insist that they try this case!"

David was bent over in his chair looking either sick or distressed. "What would have happened if we hadn't come along? Antonio has already been in prison for six years, and no one even cares that his case hasn't been tried!"

"God has something very special planned for little Antonio. He's young, perhaps he'll forget how awful life has been for him." Knowing what we do now, I could easily understand why the lawyers had wanted us to take another boy, but God had led us to Antonio and things were going to be different.

Seven days in the Mexicali valley disappeared with only a trace of evidence as proof of all the work we had done toward Antonio's release.

Our little friend hung despondently on the fence as he once again watched us leave the prison. I couldn't help feeling guilty knowing that my comfortable home and an exciting life awaited me. Antonio probably didn't have enough knowledge to fabricate a good dream; maybe he dreamed about being the toughest kid in the prison. From what Lupe said his dream would soon come true.

The vagueness that had surrounded my dealing with the original lawyers vanished when Lupe came on the case. A camaraderie spontaneously developed between us, and we moved forward aggressively. She visited Antonio regularly but found the director less and less accommodating. This inconvenience was irritating but tolerable, since we knew Antonio would soon be released.

Back at home I finally completed the American immigration papers but lacked the release papers from the Mexican government. All the documents would be sent to Washington,

D.C., and after being processed there, they would be sent to Tijuana, where we would immigrate Antonio through to the United States.

Before the release papers could be sent, however, Antonio's case would have to be tried. Lupe worked like a beaver to finagle a court date, and at last it was arranged. We had six weeks to plan our final and only defense for Antonio. Lupe's amazing confidence made me feel very relaxed, and as the trial day approached and my schedule at the university came to a crescendo, she convinced me that it wasn't necessary to attend the trial. The case was between the lawyers and the courts, and I wouldn't be called upon to testify.

My teaching was very important to me, and Lupe's suggestion came as a relief. We arranged to have Amelia stand in for me at the trial—just in case—and briefed her thoroughly on all the details.

It's very hard for me to admit feelings of anxiety, but on the morning of the trial, I could hardly find a thing to distract me from my anxious waiting. Although it was a beautiful fall morning, golden sunshine pouring through my windows, birds singing, and the aroma of fresh coffee in the air, I felt a dull ache in my stomach and an inability to concentrate on the work at my desk. Each time the phone rang I grabbed it off the cradle and expected to hear Lupe's voice. When it wasn't her, I quickly got off, trying hard not to insult anyone.

It had been over a year since we had found Antonio, and I wanted to end this nightmare for him today. But what if they tried to cover up their blunder and prove him guilty? That morning my telephone rang so many times that my heart felt like a yo-yo. At last Lupe called. "We won, Carolyn, we won! In thirty short minutes it was over, and Antonio was proven innocent."

Lupe continued while I echoed each phrase with schoolgirl excitement. "All right!" I shouted. "Praise the Lord, Antonio's innocent! We won, we won!" If only the trial could have given him back the six years he'd lost in the prison, but he was free and that's all that mattered.

"Listen to this, Carolyn," Lupe's voice sounded triumphant. "Antonio's verdict of innocent will be registered in Mexico City. He was proven innocent of the crime and will not have any kind of prison record ever, anywhere. As far as the judges are concerned, he was held illegally. Talk about exoneration! Not only is he innocent, but the authorities look very bad for neglecting an innocent child."

All of this was more than I had dared dream would happen. The slow processing had definitely dulled my anticipation, but with this news, my new plans leaped into action even while Lupe talked.

"Carolyn, I'm photocopying all the court papers and sending them to you."

"Lupe, that's great, just fantastic!" I sounded like a winning coach. "When can we get Antonio out of La Granja?"

"Today sounds perfect to me, but realistically it will be more like a month or so. Papers must be drawn up and signed, then mailed to Mexico City and recorded, then sent back to us before we can get him out. We also need to send the release papers to American Immigration in Los Angeles and then on to Washington, D.C., but you'll have to sign them first."

"Great. If you can get the papers ready, I'll come down and sign them, then we can go tell Antonio the good news right away. It would be cruel to wait a whole month to tell him!"

It took Lupe several weeks to get the final release papers from the courts, but the minute she called, I was ready to leave and very grateful to my faithful interpreter, David, for coming along as well.

The familiar ride down to Mexico afforded me a breather from my otherwise breathless routine and a good time to think about Antonio. Images of well-nurtured ten-year-old boys came to mind, and I contrasted them to the "fighter" that was soon to be released from the Mexican prison. Had six years of daily living in a boys' prison done irreparable damage? No one could erase any of the awful things he had heard and seen and, I'm sure, experienced. This boy had never known the love of a mother or a father or the natural give-and-take of a loving family. Survival was the only ethic he knew, but he would never find approval in the United States living solely by that standard. Antonio, I'm afraid, will be in for some drastic changes, I thought. Oh well, God is in this, and Antonio will make it. Happy and Jerry would certainly be perfect parents for him!

After signing the papers and accepting extravagant congratulations from the other lawyers in her office, Lupe, David, and I went directly to La Granja.

We knew only too well how the prison director felt about us since with each visit our relationship deteriorated further. Perhaps he had tolerated us initially, but now he hated us for intruding upon his neat little schemes and exposing the prison not only to Mexican criticism, but American as well.

An intense dialogue between Lupe and myself nearly caused us to walk right into the prison director. His body was obstructing the entrance, in what wasn't exactly a welcoming stance. Perhaps a Sherman tank might describe the image he projected as he stood, his feet spread apart, and gave his belt a jerk to bring his pants up over his belly. Nice try, I grinned inwardly.

His beady eyes belied his lame efforts to sound friendly. "Hello, senoritas. I'm sorry, but Antonio isn't here."

Lupe and I glanced sideways at each other, not wanting to take our eyes off the director for even a second. "Where is he?" Lupe's voice was controlled but demanding.

His nonchalance was irritating beyond endurance, but I studied his manner carefully as he spoke. "I have developed a new rehabilitation program here at La Granja, and Antonio has been placed in a very select home in Mexicali. They have several children and he will be attending public school with them. Just see how well-adjusted he will be when you get him out!"

His unconcealed sarcasm made me think he knew something we didn't. Then I realized that this tyrannical director had never believed we would get Antonio out of prison because he was prepared to stand in our way. Could it be that Antonio was a perverted kind of prize for him as director, "the youngest murderer in all of Mexico"?

Cautiously, Lupe said, "That sounds real good, but while we're here we would like to go visit him. We have some very important information for him."

He emanated an impossible cool. "No, I don't think it is wise to see the boy."

Looking him up and down, I hoped to discover a shred of integrity. David cleared his throat in a cautionary manner, and it registered with me that all three of us smelled a rat. "We have traveled over four hundred miles round trip and would really like to see Antonio!" Sternness came across loud and clear, but inside I groped miserably for an ultimatum. Actually we were at his mercy. Our persistence finally produced a scribbled address on a dirty piece of paper the director shoved at David.

"I really disapprove of this visit," he warned.

With David driving and Lupe and me crammed into the front seat beside him, we headed for the address he'd given us on the outskirts of Mexicali. Maybe we'd forgotten to thank the prison director; I wasn't sure. For an hour or so we hunted for an address that didn't exist, stopping many times to ask directions. Finally convinced that we were on a wild goose chase, we went back to La Granja for the right address.

None of us was surprised that the director was gone and the records closed to our inspection. In order to see Antonio, we would have to spend the night in Mexico again. We stayed. But it would be nice to end this routine—and all our dealings with the disagreeable director.

Early the next day, we arrived at La Granja and located the slightly embarrassed person of the prison director. "Yes, I know that was the wrong address, but you know that your visit to see Antonio displeased me very much."

It was time to pull rank on this would-be military giant. "We have some great news to tell him. His case has been tried and he has been proven innocent." The prison director looked sick; red blotches spread quickly up his neck and face as if he couldn't decide whether to blush or blanch. All at once his expression turned to one of ugly anger. "This is my program! Do you understand? And you may not see the boy! I am helping to rehabilitate him for you. He's in a good home, now, and in school. That will make it easier for him and for you when he is finally released."

I remembered the words that God had given me: "Don't take no for an answer." I didn't want to be obnoxious and I didn't want to destroy any good that our outreach program had done, but Antonio needed to hear what had happened in court. "I am sorry, sir, but we do want to see him!"

Angry eruptions of molten words met my demand, "Well, I am sorry too, because I can't let you see him. If you want to see him, you are going to have to get a court order."

"If we need a court order, sir, we'll get it!" My voice was level out of habit rather than desire. Wasn't he something?

The unpaved canal road had lost its novelty with overuse and become insignificant in view of the difficult person we dealt with each time we used it. This time we traveled thinking about Antonio and wondering where he could be today.

Back at the records office the judges greeted us as long-lost friends and seemed thrilled with the progress of Antonio's case. For several minutes we discussed Antonio; then I told them what had happened at the prison. Almost without further explanation, they issued us a court order, and we were on our way back to La Granja. Knowing how difficult court orders are to obtain, the prison director must have felt he had effectively handled our intrusion for some time. When he saw that we had returned in a mere two hours, we became a formidable opposition.

Our aggressive approach made him squirm. He realized that something had gone wrong with his plan and tried to call up his commanding spirit by folding his arms over his chest and assuming a bored expression. Silently, Lupe handed him the court order. The despairing man's nerve was finally broken. "I'm sorry. I don't know where he is." He immediately walked into his office and shut and locked the door behind him.

My mouth actually fell open, and I heard Lupe saying, "Something is wrong here, Carolyn. I don't know what it is, but I'll find out and give you a call at home."

Emptiness mocked our endless hours of labor, and cords of uncertainty threatened to strangle my optimism as we left the prison that day. Staying longer in Mexico was out of the question. Things were piling up at the university, and I had to get back to work and my classes. David and I dragged ourselves back and would have felt utterly defeated if it hadn't been for the cathartic conversation we kept up all the way home.

Time after time my inexperienced intern lawyer had impressed me with her efficiency, if not yet her complete success. The very next day I was sitting in my office when Lupe called.

"Hello Carolyn, I found out what happened. That contemptible prison director has been selling boys to a slave labor ring and not only pocketing the money for their sale but also the money he's given from the government to keep the boys at the prison. I'm so sorry, Carolyn, but Antonio has been sold as a child slave."

Chapter Ten

"Sold into slave labor?" My heart fell like a broken elevator. Could it be true? After all these years of sitting in that rotten prison, Antonio had disappeared on the eve of his release. My soaring hopes crashed, and my dreams for Antonio vanished with Lupe's words. "Lupe, where is he, who was he sold to? This is ridiculous; let's go get him!"

"This must be very difficult for you to hear, Carolyn, and I'm sorry. No one knows where to find Antonio because the director didn't keep any records. He apparently sold nearly half the boys out of this prison, and he can't remember anything except how much money he collected. Believe me, Carolyn," Lupe assured me, "I'll stay on this case until Antonio is found. I need to be very honest with you; this is not the first time I've heard about child slaves around here. You should be prepared for bad news, although I pray not. We may not find him at all—or alive!"

Lupe's words penetrated like a bolt of lightning. Yesterday I was going to tell Antonio that he would be legally free in just a few weeks, then I was told that he was living with a lovely Mexican family. Now—he's been sold as a child slave and may be dead.

"I'll keep in touch, Carolyn, and the minute something comes up, you'll be the first to hear." I hung up the telephone but left my hand on the receiver; it seemed like a tiny link to Antonio, and it was hard to let go. Sinking deep into my chair, an avalanche of misery buried me in an icy grave of grief. Antonio was gone, and I couldn't believe the empty loneliness I felt! This episode clinched my growing feelings for him. His sparkling eyes, his eager expression, his neat little brown hands were almost tangible memories, strong reminders that he was very important to me. I really loved that little kid!

Over the years I had learned that God was changeless, reasonable, and loving. Not only did he love me but he loved Antonio as well. Pleading with my God, I asked question after question, then begged for Antonio's safety. This had been a very long and difficult year and a half, and I longed for the assurance that it hadn't been wasted. Once again, God had led my wrestling spirit full circle to the fact that I must trust him. With this fresh on my mind, I realized that Antonio was completely out of my control and that my commitment to God was completely *in* my control. I made my choices.

Immediately charged, I telephoned David, Happy and Jerry, and everyone else I could think of, and we all prayed. The word was spread quickly, and soon many hundreds of people were praying for Antonio—for his safety . . . for his life.

Considering the endless steps in the immigration process that we had already taken, it seemed as though we should be finished. Not so! There were still more details, and I decided it would be best to continue just as if Antonio were still in the prison.

Over the next several months, my phone rang constantly with inquiries about Antonio. Lupe and I stayed in close contact, and she kept me informed about possible leads on Antonio's whereabouts.

The despicable prison director was interrogated by the Juvenile Court and the governor's office and lost his job. Lupe told us that the new prison director was doing a wonderful job of cleaning up the prison.

Months slipped by and still there was no clue to Antonio; he was simply gone. Another Easter vacation rolled around, and the Mexicali Outreach teams headed south. Nine hundred high school and college kids from several states made up this year's strong teams, a respectable challenge for any director. Every year God blessed us bigger and better. It had been two years since we had discovered Antonio, and La Granja had drastically changed, even though the young prisoners were generally the same. The bunk beds were still rammed tightly together, but each one had a mattress, blanket, and bedspread. The old toilet was as clean as possible and had a new seat and a tile floor covering the old dirt one. An old black-and-white television set hung from the middle of the room. I asked David if he could find the familiar fifty-gallon drum of drinking water, but fortunately it was gone.

The songs and stories of the team, and the rapt attention of the young audience, reminded me of that similar visit two years ago. I found myself scanning the crowded room for Antonio. I knew he wasn't at La Granja, of course, but I couldn't help wishing he were. What an irony: to be wishing him into prison when we'd fought so hard to get him out! I prayed again—as I prayed so often—that he was safe, that whoever had him had been moved to gentleness by his vulnerability, not to brutality.

So many people had fallen in love with Antonio, and now he was gone. Had God used him and us to get rid of the corrupt prison director and get the prison cleaned up? That was okay, but I just couldn't believe that Antonio was gone. Envisioning his face, the little cross around his neck, even his dirty tennies, made tears fill my eyes and my heart ache for him. Again, I prayed for his safety and that he wasn't being abused. Maybe he was better off where he was than in the prison.

Great things continued to happen with our Mexicali Outreach teams and I was thankful, but everything reminded me of Antonio—he filled all my thoughts.

When the American immigration and home study processes were finally completed, I felt relieved. However, they could not be signed until Antonio was located. So while days and months rolled indifferently by, the papers sat. This waiting period was trying for Lupe, too, as the completed Mexican immigration papers sat teasingly at her elbow.

Except for a steady outpouring of concerned calls from all over the States, my life remained hectically normal. My work, personal studies, and social life were increasingly successful, and I was at peace with God. Everything was perfect except for the sweet, haunting face of a little Mexican orphan who caused a dull pain in my heart. "God, where is he? Will I ever see him again?" Sometimes I just prayed that everyone else would keep praying.

The waiting began to get to me. At times I questioned God's purpose. As the months dragged on, a real softening took place in my heart and I instinctively reached out to Antonio. It was true that sometimes relationships just clicked; I realized that it was fun for me to be with Antonio. I sensed a bond developing between us, even though he still was missing.

As if counting off the days of a prison sentence myself, I always knew how long Antonio had been missing. We had found him two and a half years ago, and he'd been missing for nine months. It was now July, and the heat of the morning promised a smoldering afternoon. I decided to see how much could be accomplished early. Domestic chores and conference planning combined kept me busy inside and out and upstairs and down. The phone rang and I answered it as casually as picking lint off my dark brown carpet. A man's voice in a very heavy Mexican accent spoke words to this effect: "Are you Carolyn Koons, the lady who's interested in the adoption of Antonio Hernandez Sanchez?"

This was a new one; what could it mean? Stumbling over my own words, I quickly answered, "Yes, yes, I am!"

"Senorita, are you still interested in the boy?"

"I definitely am! Have you heard from him?"

"Yes, senorita! He has just been placed back into La Granja prison, and you better come for him quickly if you don't want him to disappear again." Click! Dazed, and wondering if I'd dreamed it, I listened to the dial tone. Who could that have been? Armando, the woodshop teacher and guard at the prison? But why would he have hung up so quickly?

A friend from church who had a private plane had once offered to help out in a pinch. As I dialed his number, I prayed he'd meant it. He had. I gathered up all the necessary legal documents and met him at the airport.

Amelia was waiting at the other end. As a precaution, she'd sent several people from her mission to La Granja to keep an eye on Antonio; and she had stopped at Lupe's office to pick up the signed prison release papers. We had to think and move fast. As much as I wanted to see Antonio, we decided it would be best for me to hand-deliver the Mexican papers to the American immigration office immediately and get them in the mail by 5:00 P.M. So we exchanged documents, and I flew home while Amelia went on to La Granja to secure Antonio's release. She planned to hide him in a friend's home in a remote village several miles below Mexicali until I could return for him.

Back in Glendora, I jumped into my car and raced to the American immigration office in downtown Los Angeles. Mrs. Myers was extremely pleased to see me and efficiently looked over the papers from La Granja, the courts, the juvenile judges, and the lawyer's office, checking each for an official signature. I held my breath. "Congratulations, Carolyn! Everything is here and signed. We'll mail these to Washington, D.C., today. They'll look them over, put an official stamp on each one, and send them to Mexico. They should arrive in Tijuana at the American Consulate in exactly seven days, and then you can immigrate Antonio into the United States."

I could have left my car and flown home on my own power. These words were barely believable after the barren desert of waiting I had just gone through. In seven days Antonio would be free to come to the United States—innocent of all criminal charges. Thank God, we were on track now.

My telephone had certainly been the herald of significant news lately, and once again I stayed home awaiting a call from Amelia. Had she been able to get Antonio out of prison and into a safe hiding place? I waited and thought back over my incredibly long day, beginning with the strange phone call from the Mexican man. It was breathlessly hot; I wanted a shower badly but didn't dare risk missing Amelia's call.

The phone rang, ending my impatient vigil. Amelia's reassuring words refreshed me more than a million cool showers, "We've got him, Carolyn, and he's safe."

The celebration couldn't start just yet. "How does he look, Amelia?"

"He looks great. You ought to see him. He is so excited to be with us."

"Thanks, Amelia. I'm so happy. This is fantastic! Tell Antonio that I said hi and that we'll come for him in a week."

A possessive feeling about Antonio gave me a weird sensation as I dialed Happy and Jerry, Antonio's soon-to-be mom and dad. They were wildly happy about Antonio's release and realized that God had worked a beautiful miracle. But as we went into the actual details for Antonio's adoption, some serious obstacles surfaced and made us move ahead with caution. About now I noticed that my mind was going in a thousands different directions at about a million miles an hour. To say the least, I was overstimulated and emotional.

In the two and a half years since we had found Antonio a lot had happened in Happy and Jerry's lives. They had a beautiful baby son, and Happy was pregnant again, due any day. They had their hands full. Jerry's new job was the real concern, however. He had recently accepted a county job: they were both now live-in house parents for fifteen very tough delinquent boys Antonio's age. Jerry expressed serious concern about putting Antonio into this institutional environment. He was absolutely right; Antonio needed the undivided attention of an adult in order to make a good adjustment. He didn't need to move in with fifteen other boys his age, all with their own problems. We talked for a long time, just as we had done numerous times over the past months, and even years, concerning Antonio's future. As we began to see God's leading in their lives—and in mine—over the past couple of years, we began to see a different plan for Antonio's life developing from the one we had started out with. Maybe one of the reasons it had taken two and a half years to get Antonio out of prison was that it had taken that long for the necessary changes to take place in all our lives—especially mine!

During the last moments of my conversation with Happy and Jerry, I glanced down at the official papers spread out on the table before me. In all the rush of the day, I had failed to look at them closely. Now my eyes rested on the most shocking words I had ever read. Clearly printed and officially notarized was the name *Antonio Koons.* Finished with my telephone conversation, I hung up the phone and sat there dazed.

It was true that I loved Antonio and that the thought of giving him to Happy and Jerry or anyone else was really beginning to bother me. But I was thirty-five years old and single, with no plans for marriage. In no way did my lifestyle include a little boy, especially one who needed an exceptional amount of attention. Aside from a structured teaching schedule, my life was absolutely unpredictable and wonderful. My schedule was always packed with activity and excitement, and I often left town on a moment's notice for some new adventure.

But denying the work that God had done in my life these last two years would be impossible, for loving Antonio had softened my heart and was making me a different person. I must be insane to even consider adopting Antonio.

I quickly pushed all these thoughts aside and made a list of friends that I thought could take—or would even consider taking—Antonio. During the next couple of days I contacted them all—without a solution. I shouldn't have been surprised; how many people would consider adopting a boy who had spent over seven years of his life in prison, for murder!

It was only a few days before I would pick up Antonio, and still there wasn't even a prospective home for him. I was too panicked to sleep. I had lain awake that night torn by internal conflict. The night was spent, and so was I. This was a private moment, my draperies were still closed, and I was in my robe and slippers feeling bruised and very tired. My breakfast nook was very cozy, so, hoping to revive myself after a sleepless night, I snuggled in and nursed a cup of steaming coffee. Stacks of official papers still covered the table. Finally, taking one very significant paper in hand, I read the name "Antonio Koons" again.

"God, is this what you planned for me all along? I asked you to change my life, but I never dreamed you would ask me to do this! But if this is what you want, God—even though it sounds ridiculous to me—I'll become Antonio's mother."

Chapter Eleven

God had pulled rank on me before, and I keenly appreciated his ability to produce in me qualities beyond even my wildest expectations. But motherhood was light years away from my ambitious, career-oriented goals. Me, a mother! The whole idea was so bizarre that just saying the word *mother* seemed to cauterize my freedom. Feelings of excitement and mild terror swept over me as I thought about what I had done.

During the days that remained in that memorable week I tried to prepare myself for motherhood, thinking that it would be nice to have the usual nine months but very glad to have skipped the Mother Goose and diapering days. I'm sure that God gave me much more credit than I gave myself. A crash course in mothering might have helped, but there wasn't time; in five days *my* house would be *our* house. Having another person around would definitely be the biggest adjustment I would have to make. For most of my thirty-five years I'd lived alone, in the perfect bliss of having things the way I like them —neat. Even during college I had had my own dorm room, though I spent very little time in it because there was always the show, dinner with friends, or someone to visit. Staying home night after night with a little boy was a terrifying thought, but perhaps he would have a free spirit similar to mine and we would have some great adventures together. The thought crossed my mind that Antonio might actually teach me a thing or two.

Instinctively I sensed a storm and reasoned that if proper protective measures were taken in advance, a storm could be enjoyable. So with pad and pencil I headed for the condominium swimming pool to sit and write on my customary check-off list all the problems that Antonio and I might face. The sparkling blue of the water and the lovely overhanging oak trees went unnoticed by me that afternoon as my own thoughts left little room for anything else.

Flashbacks of some of my travels entertained me first. Three different times I had traveled all over Europe and at other times visited Russia, Czechoslovakia, and Poland, including the Auschwitz concentration camps. Right then, I nearly called my friends and packed my bags, remembering the exciting times we had shared bicycling in the Swiss Alps, shooting rapids in canoes and rafts, climbing the Eiffel Tower, and backpacking in the mountains. Surely Antonio would fit right into my life. But what if he didn't?

Culture shock was inevitable for Antonio. Just getting used to brown carpet instead of brown mud between his toes would be a major adjustment. Then there was school. Where do you start at twelve years old with very little school behind you? Kindergarten? Sixth grade?

How would Antonio and I communicate? His english was nonexistent and I had never learned Spanish. Sign language would be adequate for explaining which room was his, how to turn on the water, but how would we talk about intangibles like faith and morality? Teaching Antonio morals could be a major project, considering the amoral environment that he had been part of for so long. We'd have a lot to cover. But perhaps there were things better left unspoken: only God could understand what Antonio had been through, and bring comfort.

Having thought through these issues I felt somewhat more prepared to deal with them. I hated to be caught off guard. Now that the big day had arrived, I timidly crawled out of bed and walked around the house in my robe. I loved my house and my life the way they were, and a fearfully uncertain future threatened to change everything. But I began to think that I was ready for some change.

If I were to be a mother, my good friend Alva Peters would have to be a grandmother. I had come to value Alva particularly at holidays for her traditional baking and decorating—but most of all for her unusual ability to make a warm and loving home for anyone who needed to be loved. The Peterses' home in Twain Harte, near the base of the mountains, where Alva's husband, Russell, pastors a thriving church, had long given stability to my life as a single; now it would do the same for Antonio. It wasn't without precedent; Alva had cared for foster children in addition to her own four (it was through her youngest son, Steve, then a student at APU, that I had become acquainted with the family), so she was to some extent prepared for her role. Before I'd received this latest news about Antonio, Alva had already agreed to accompany me to Mexicali—for moral support. I broke the news of her "grandparenthood" as soon as she arrived. She was delighted with my decision and promised to help create a family for Antonio.

Among the many changes that had taken place while we tried to free Antonio was David Johnson's marriage to Sue. Both of them agreed to accompany me, along with Alva, to pick up Antonio.

Our drive to Mexicali had a different feeling about it than previous trips. With fear and trembling, I pictured a little boy hiding in a tiny house in Mexico awaiting the arrival of his mother. Antonio's mother, that's me. "Oh, dear God, talk to me, tell me that I'm doing the right thing." Then I remembered something Dr. Grant had said over two years ago: "Carolyn, this is the craziest caper you've ever tried, but that little kid is very lucky to have a friend like you." It's easy to be a good friend; God help me to be a good mother!

A whirlwind of thought kept me isolated from my friends as we drove along drenched in the perspiration of a summer heat wave. As the ebb of fearfulness gave way to the flow of excitement, new thoughts flooded in. "Hey, you guys, I'm going to pick up my son! I've lived alone long enough; today I'm getting a new son and we'll continue our journey together." Everyone cheered supportively and feelings of optimism revived me again.

A lot of people back home had said that they would step

in and help me with Antonio—sort of group parenting. In my naiveté it sounded good. Parenting would be okay because I planned to really work on it and had loads of friends to help me. Anyway, Antonio would love me and trust me and appreciate me for all that I had done for him. At least I could count on that! Precious little did I know about what lay ahead for me in our journey!

In temperatures of 112–115 degrees, we bumped and rattled down the unpaved road to the village where we were to find Antonio. There was Amelia in obviously high spirits waving to us as we stopped. "You go ahead, I'll be along in a minute," I suggested. So Alva, David, and Sue got out of the car and greeted Amelia while I frantically tried to calm a sudden rush of panic. I needed just a few minutes of space. Since we had first discovered Antonio, I had seen him only a few times. Would he be the same little boy that I remembered so well sitting with sparkling eyes and radiant face in the front row of our program at the prison? What if he doesn't do crazy things to my heart anymore? Maybe I won't even know him. Maybe he won't like me!

I forced myself to get out of the car and join the others. Amelia threw loving arms around me, and it was her hug and encouraging happiness that helped me take the next step.

"Carolyn, everything's going to be fantastic. Antonio's had a good week here in the village, and he can hardly wait to see you." Amelia led the way into the house. Children seemed to be everywhere, and a grandmother sat in a chair by the door. Everyone was giggling about something. "Is Antonio here, or out playing somewhere?" I asked, straining my eyes to see in the darkened room.

Before Amelia could answer, David was saying—in Spanish, of course—"Hi, Antonio! How are you, tiger?" He and Sue squeezed through between three double beds that crowded the tiny room and stood beside him.

Antonio raised a bandaged foot toward me. "What's this, Antonio?" I looked at Amelia.

"He was playing in the canal this morning and cut his foot on a can or something," she explained. "It's pretty bad, you'll see."

By now my eyes had adjusted to the dimness of the room, and I could clearly see Antonio's face. Only God knows how close I came to singing the "Hallelujah Chorus" that very moment. For there before me were two sparkling eyes, a huge grin, and a little boy who immediately melted my heart. I met his grin with mine and experienced an incredible relief as I opened my heart to my son. He was so happy to see me; without hesitating, he got up, hobbled to the corner of the room, and from beneath a bed pulled a tiny, dilapidated suitcase. Then he untied the rope that held it together, disclosing all his earthly possessions: one worn-out pair of shorts, two threadbare T-shirts, and something that needed explanation. It was a three-foot length of string tied to a rusty old six-volt battery. "What's this?" David inquired.

"Mi coche, mi coche." Antonio's toy meant a lot to him; I could tell by the inflections of his voice.

David sat down beside him. "Your car, huh? That's great, Antonio." So David and Antonio shared some "man talk" briefly while we waited.

Eventually, David encouraged Antonio to put his things away, we should be going. Antonio swung the rope attached to his fancy little suitcase over his shoulder and, with a smile as big as the sun, started toward the car.

One final matter of business remained before we could head home. Lupe would be leaving on vacation the next day, so we drove directly to her office to pick up the necessary adoption papers. She had asked that we come for the papers after we picked up Antonio so that she could see him. The professional air of the lawyer's office lit the fires of interest under Antonio as he studied every detail of his surroundings.

Upon entering Lupe's office, he was nearly smothered with affectionate attention. This was a huge victory in Lupe's professional life and a joyous day for her personally; she had grown to love Antonio very much. Lupe pulled Antonio close to her chair and left her arm around his waist as she talked. "Carolyn, here are your papers, just sign the bottom line and make a decision about this date."

I took the paper. "What day do I need to make a decision about?"

Her manner was light and snappy as she told us, "His birthday! When would you like to celebrate his birthday?"

We all laughed in relief, but Alva expressed our feelings. "This is going to be fun. Carolyn's made so many weighty decisions lately that it would be fun to plan a birthday party."

Antonio missed the comments spoken in English and looked around the room at five laughing adults, hoping for a clue. David explained everything to him.

"Thanks, David. What am I going to do without you?" Then I turned, "How fun, Lupe. I love the idea of choosing Antonio's birthday. How about today, July eighteenth?"

"Good! Now, how old do you want him to be, eleven, twelve, or thirteen?" We all looked at each other, by now in uproarious laughter. "The doctors estimated him to be around twelve. Do you want him to turn twelve today, or thirteen today?" Lupe's questions seemed delightfully frivolous. How many parents get to choose the exact day and year of their child's birth?

"Let's make him twelve today. That will help us with school later," I responded.

Lupe turned Antonio so that he faced her. "Antonio, today is your birthday, and I'm going to write it here on this line to show that you were born July eighteenth in 1965. From now on, every single year on July eighteenth you will have a birthday."

Antonio was usually speechless, expressing his feelings with his eyes; by this time they had outgrown their sockets. He pointed to the freshly written date and softly said in Spanish, "My birthday." It took several blinks for me to bring my teary eyes into focus. I'll never forget that moment of priceless joy.

Thoughtfully anticipating all our needs, Lupe had prepared a folder filled with important papers. "Here are all the documents you need, Carolyn. I'll be leaving tomorrow for Mexico City, so I guess this is the last that we'll see each other for a while. Let me thank you for letting me be part of this very special case, and especially for today. You're all wonderful people! And you have a very powerful God. Have a good trip to your new home, Antonio." Then she looked over at me, "Are you leaving for home right now?"

"No," I nodded in Antonio's direction. "First we're going to do a little shopping, then get a good night's rest at the hotel. We have to immigrate Antonio through at Tijuana and that will be a long, very hot drive."

We all stood to leave, but Lupe and I took a moment to search each other's faces and share a million unspoken thoughts and feelings. Words could never adequately express the bottomless depth of our feeling of kinship. We embraced, then left Lupe in her office. The mood was set, and the celebration was already in full swing for a very special little man's birthday.

Our next stop was a small clothing store, where we purchased a light brown pair of pants, some jeans, about five T-shirts, and some underwear and socks. I encouraged Antonio to choose the T-shirts that he liked best, but looking through the large selection on the rack, he became overwhelmed. When I narrowed the choices to a few, he did much better and was able to zero in on one that had a dolphin pictured on the front and lettering that read, Sea World, San Diego, California. That was his very favorite. It was nearly impossible for him to try on clothes, because of his swollen foot and filthy body. I was eager to get him showered, and he was eager for everything.

La Granja had been a limited and sterile environment for Antonio's quick mind; now that he was free, absolutely nothing escaped his curious stares.

We had accommodations at the lovely Hotel Lucerna in Mexicali. Everyone helped Antonio with his packages of new clothes and his old suitcase, while I helped him hobble along on his now very sore foot. It was fun being this close to him as he reacted to the beautiful swimming pool, the white-coated waiters, and the well-ordered grounds. Our party shared large adjoining rooms that further impressed him.

Alva busied herself cutting the tags from Antonio's new clothes while I asked David to help him shower for dinner. Antonio seemed agreeable enough and went into the bathroom. Alva, David, Sue, and I were sitting on the beds talking a million miles an hour when Sue noticed that the shower wasn't running yet.

I didn't know what to think. "David, will you please check on him?"

"Sure, maybe his foot hurts too badly, poor kid." So David knocked on the door, and it slowly opened. David went inside and closed the door. It was quite some time before he emerged, displaying a grin of fatherly amusement. "He didn't know anything—how to start the shower or adjust any of the knobs. He was just standing there looking around at everything as though he had discovered a big new world. Then David had the nerve to laugh and say to me, "Good luck, Carolyn. I'd love to see some of the things that you two get into!"

We chatted away for another twenty minutes before Sue gave David a little punch in the ribs and said, "The shower's been running for twenty minutes. Do you think there's any hot water left?"

Alva was quick. "He's probably trying to squeeze twelve years' worth of showers into one. That's very nice, now you all just leave him alone!"

David roared in laughter, "Carolyn, I hope you have a huge hot water heater! I'll go check on him." David was in the bathroom with him for a long time, talking, but mostly laughing. They were really having a good time. At last, the door opened and the new Antonio Koons stepped out, complete in tan-colored pants and a dark brown shirt. Obviously, David had helped him comb his hair, which was neatly slicked back, perfectly framing his gigantic smile.

"Glory be!" Alva said, and I reached for my camera.

"Antonio, you're so handsome. Tell him, David!" I took several pictures, and Antonio drank up the attention like dry sand. The thought crossed my mind that it was fun to love Antonio.

"Is anyone hungry? Let's go to dinner." It had been a very exciting day, and I wondered if Antonio would be able to eat at all.

At dinner, the newlyweds sat side by side, and Grandma Alva and I sat on either side of Antonio. Again, he was already caught up with a new environment, inspecting every detail of the white-clothed table and its fine setting.

After we offered our blessing, we all noticed Antonio staring at the basket of dinner rolls the waiter had brought when he took our order. With great effort he tore his eyes from the rolls and asked me if he could have one. Alva passed him a roll but within minutes he asked for another one and then a third. We stopped him at two, knowing that dinner would soon be ready, but it was hard; he was obviously starved.

Within a few minutes our bountiful meal was served. The sizzling hot broiled steak, the baked potato swimming in creamy butter, and the variety of fresh vegetables that sat before Antonio sent steamy little fingers of aroma right into his face and begged him to eat. He didn't realized that four adults were enjoying his every move much more than their own meal. We all watched as he filled his lungs, smelling the delicious foods, and then cautiously looked to me for direction. Carefully, I exaggerated proper table manners to give Antonio his cues. He proved to be a quick study and handled himself very well. At least he seemed to want to do the right thing.

Each of us tried to include Antonio in our conversation, but usually he just grinned and answered simply *si,* or *no.* His stuttering seemed to inhibit lengthy conversation, but I was convinced that he felt comfortable.

Dinner finished, we pushed our plates aside and sat back,

more than satisfied. Only then did I notice that Antonio was still reaching for dinner rolls. His plate was completely empty; how could he hold another bite? Then I realized what he was doing. He was stuffing his pockets with the rolls as if this would be his last chance to eat—ever!

It was nice to be able to speak English and know that Antonio couldn't understand that we were talking about him. We all decided that he was eating for lost time, just as he had showered. "Oh great," I groaned, "I'll have the cleanest, fattest son in town!"

Alva defended him again, "Stop teasing, the boy is starved. Just look at his skinny arms!" Of course, she was right, Antonio needed to eat, but we all laughed anyway just because we were so happy and relieved to have Antonio with us.

While Antonio was taking his leisurely shower earlier, I had called the restaurant and ordered a birthday cake. As the waiter walked through the dining area with the cake, I grabbed my camera and hoped that Antonio wouldn't die of all the excitement. A birthday cake with candles was set before a very surprised boy, and we began to sing "Happy Birthday to you, Happy Birthday to you . . ." His eyes danced with delight, and he welcomed our congratulatory hugs. Antonio paused to make a wish, just as David had instructed him, then huskily blew out every candle.

I already knew that Antonio loved presents and really looked forward to giving him a gift. Grandma Alva presented the first gift, a yellow T-shirt with "Antonio" printed across the front. He was thrilled and posed cheerfully for several pictures. Our next was a set of four tiny cars, and when Antonio got through the wrapping paper of this gift, he shot out of his chair with excitement. He simply couldn't believe it. I think that we had just made him the happiest boy in the world. We hoped the cars would occupy him during our long drive home.

Finally, I reached into my purse and pulled out a small, wrapped box. By this time the rivers of love and acceptance ran high, and Antonio carefully reached out for the gift. His look of tenderness and gratitude toward me made me want to give him much more—perhaps a little part of me. But isn't that what a true gift represents?

He had a real treasure and wanted the thrill of receiving it to last forever. As if lost in the magic spell, he gently caressed the package, and at last he carefully unwrapped it, revealing a little calculator inside. Tears came to his eyes, and he hugged me and kissed my cheek.

Antonio remembered perfectly our conversation in the prison about him coming to the United States and receiving a calculator. It was a symbol between us, rich with meaning. I wondered if anyone had ever kept a promise to him before.

Antonio's twelfth birthday had been very special. We had laughed a lot, eaten plenty—including cake and ice cream—and watched Antonio enjoy his presents. We had watched him eat everything he could get his hands on, as if he'd never eat again, and walk away from the table with rolls bulging from his pockets.

It was good to crawl into bed that night beneath the crisp white sheets. This had been one of the biggest days of my life. July 18, 1977, I had become a mother.

Just before falling asleep I glanced toward Antonio's cot and laughed to see the flashing of his calculator light from under his sheet. Yes, Antonio, that calculator does mean that you're coming to the United States, but not just for a visit. Antonio Koons, you're coming as my son.

Chapter Twelve

Even though my body was desperately tired, anxiety about Antonio's future kept sleep at bay all night. I worried about everything from his lack of a toothbrush to his college education. He had no such problems; within a few minutes, he had dropped off to sleep. I tiptoed over and turned off the calculator. In spite of the horrors he'd seen, tonight, at least, his sleep was untroubled. He looked angelic.

There were still many questions that remained unanswered. Perhaps every new mother goes through this questioning time. What was he going to be like to live with day after day? How could I keep up a pretense of confidence twenty-four hours a day? Could I ever let my hair down again? My fearful thoughts reached long arms into the future. Maybe I'll even be a grandmother someday.

One thing was for certain: there was no turning back; this was for keeps. A strange gutsy feeling of determination came over me as, once again, I resolved to follow God's leading, one step at a time. "Spare me a nervous breakdown between steps, dear Lord."

Before I'd slept, the alarm went off; it was 5:30 in the morning. Everyone quickly arose, and soon the car was packed and we were gathered for a hearty breakfast. Again, I really didn't expect Antonio to eat, remembering how he'd gorged himself the night before, but he made quick work of the eggs, bacon, and toast he was served, then continued to stuff himself with rolls. No one's leftovers were wasted that morning, either, thanks to Antonio! With bulging pockets, he half-waddled, half-hobbled, away from the table, very miserably full.

The road to Tijuana was narrow, steep, winding, incredibly hot, and very long—a four-hour trip. None of us looked forward to the trip, despite our eagerness to complete Antonio's immigration process. Only a short way up the road Antonio became very still and, within a few minutes, asked David to stop. Instantly, he bolted from the car and lost his breakfast along the side of the road.

Back in the car, Antonio was soon sound asleep leaning against David's arm. I was glad he could escape the misery of the long mountain road and hoped he would sleep a long time.

The expected temperature was 115, so it seemed wise to baby the car and guard against overheating. Greatly to our relief, we did make it over the mountains, and once into Tijuana, we easily found the American Consulate.

The Director of Immigration, Mr. Solomon, received us into his office. He had been expecting us. He was unassuming in appearance—short, balding, a little paunchy and somewhere in his forties—but friendly.

"Please come in," he said. "Your papers have arrived from Washington, D.C., and have been sitting here," he patted the envelope on top of his desk, "for several days. My, they processed these papers fast." I nodded, and he continued, "Mrs. Meyers from the Los Angeles immigration office notified me that the papers were on the way." Reaching down to shake Antonio's hand, he said, "So this is the lucky boy that I've been told so much about!" Antonio seemed to understand Mr. Solomon and smiled proudly.

Mr. Solomon asked to be introduced to everyone and carried on a lively conversation for a few minutes. "Well, it looks like you should be home in a few hours, Antonio. Let's have a look at your papers." With his familiarity with the task, Mr. Solomon shuffled through the documents. Truly, he should have worn gloves and handled them with great respect, they represented endless hours of my life. Then the bomb: "Carolyn, where's his passport?"

"Passport? Of course, I thought we'd get that here at your office."

"No, I'm sorry," he shook his head and spoke quietly, "You must get a passport at a passport office. You do have his birth certificate with you, in order to prove his age?" An uneasy glance passed between David and myself.

An explanation surely would resolve this problem and we could be on our way. "Sir, his mother never registered him, so the courts had us pick the date for his birthday. Can we use the court papers as a birth certificate?"

"That would be very unusual; I've never seen it done." We sensed his concern.

Almost too late, I pulled the stops on my reserve of courage and tried to be calm and controlled. "We're going to give it a try. Where is the passport office?"

Now I understood, in part, his look of concern, as he painfully explained, "The passport office and all legal documents are housed back in Mexicali."

Dark silence stole away our lightheartedness, and I carefully didn't speak for a moment. Right then the thought of driving back over those mountains was unbearable.

"I'm so sorry, Carolyn! The passport is all you lack to immigrate Antonio. If you do come back, I promise to process your papers that same day."

That "if" comment from Mr. Solomon bothered me. He acted as if he would never see us again. But with that deflating comment, we left his office in search of a restaurant; our boy must be starved again.

Over lunch we concocted an idea; David and I left Sue, Alva, and Antonio and drove to San Diego to the Mexican Consulate. There, we tried to get Antonio's passport but were told that we would definitely need to go back to Mexicali because Antonio was still in Mexico.

Back in Tijuana I faced another problem: David and Sue had to be back at work the next day—without fail. So it was with trumped-up courage that we put them on a Greyhound bus and waved good-bye. Our seemingly impossible day took on monumental proportions without the help of our only interpreter. "God, lead the way!"

The three of us spent a restless, hot night in a Tijuana hotel, rose early, and reluctantly, with Antonio sandwiched between us, started the car back over the mountains toward Mexicali. This was crazy, just crazy. I never did fumbling, stupid things like this. How could we have gotten into this mess? Why hadn't we caught the passport problem earlier?

In the hot, dusty car, silence replaced the singing and laughter of our earlier trip. Occasionally, Alva and I spoke in low serious tones, but that was all. The miles rolled by and my tension eased a bit. I would take the required steps and move on.

But Antonio didn't understand any of what was happening. My own concerns had distracted me, but now I looked down at him. He sat close to me, leaning forward, but held his body absolutely rigid. Little wrinkles creased his tan face in a look of confusion, perhaps terror. "Alva, maybe he thinks that we're taking him back to La Granja!" I couldn't imagine what a horrible thought that must have been for him.

Frantically, Alva and I tried to piece together enough Spanish words to tell Antonio that we were just picking up a missing paper and then heading home. None of our efforts seemed to relieve his despair. Then, to compound his misery, he got car sick repeatedly. We worked as best we could to comfort my worried, sick son.

As we came to the top of the ridge, Mexicali lay beyond, sweltering at 115 degrees. Our car kept overheating, but I was too tired to react. A noise from the car's engine alerted Antonio to trouble, and he perked up attentively to listen. I simply moaned. "Alva, car trouble would be too much!"

Alva's normally tidy dark hair, sprinkled with grandmotherly gray, clung damply around her face. Her lips were parched, but a rosy flush made me think how good she looked. I would have been concerned for her, except for the strength in her voice when she spoke. "Since the passport office closes at two, let's hurry over there, then look after the car."

I agreed. Without the passport we weren't going anywhere. "There's a policeman. We can get directions from him —I hope."

The policeman was almost as bilingual as we were, and we

got nowhere fast. I asked several passers-by to interpret for us and eventually got directions. I felt pressed into a box made of confusion and stuffed with obstacles. We had an hour and a half before the office closed.

All the official offices were being moved to a new, modern five-story complex on the *other* side of town. No matter where we went, where we wanted to be was on the *other side of town*. The passport office was on the third floor and was typical of the offices we'd seen: hot, stuffy rooms, long lines, and crying babies. Inching our way through the crowded room to the far end, we asked to see the director. A handsome gentleman soon came to our aid. "May I help you?" he asked pleasantly.

"Yes, thank you. My name is Carolyn Koons; this is my friend Mrs. Peters and my son, Antonio." (He probably thinks I'm crazy by now, the way I've dragged him all over Mexico.) I laid the papers on the counter and began explaining our situation.

"So you need a passport. Let me see your papers. Yes, yes, yes," he said, flipping through the documents. "Everything looks just fine; but wait, I don't see a birth certificate." He frowned.

"The court didn't have a birth certificate, so they registered his birthday as July eighteenth in 1965. See, here, on these documents." I must have looked pathetic to him, for he spoke with great kindness.

"Senorita Koons, I'm very sorry; without a birth certificate or certificate of abandonment we cannot give Antonio, or anyone else, for that matter, a passport. All birth certificates are registered in the old office complex on the other side of town." He drew up a map and sent us on our way.

The somewhat air-conditioned building we left only made the inferno on the sidewalk seem worse. "Alva, if we hurry now, maybe we can get out of here first thing in the morning. Are you up to heading across town again?"

"I'd hate to give up now when we're so close to settling this mess. Sure, let's go." I knew she was being tough for my sake; we were all tired to the bone.

The car's engine knocked and sputtered every inch of the way across town, making me think that each block would be its last. Miraculously, we did make it across town to a very familiar section. It was here that our Mexicali Outreach teams came to buy candy for the village children, but not in July.

Between the car and the second floor where we were headed there were open meat and produce markets, piled garbage and litter at the roadside, and countless numbers of people milling around. Getting out of the car, smells of every description assaulted my nostrils, then a thick wall of heat nearly pushed me back into the car. Was anything going to be without effort today? Even our walk to the office required discipline.

Worse than any previous office, the registration office was jammed with people, the air insufferably hot and unbelievably still. Taking the role of trail blazer, I led the way through the crowd, expecting Alva and Antonio to follow. Suddenly, I realized that he wasn't between us and, in a panic, started searching the room.

Just as I saw him listlessly slump onto a bench, Alva explained, "I'm sure that Antonio's more than car sick. He seems to have a fever. I think his foot's infected."

"I'll bet you're right, Alva. Let's get this birth certificate and get him back to the hotel."

Again, I asked for the director and got an immediate response. I gave a straightforward explanation of our plight, which by this time sounded like a well-rehearsed speech. The director compliantly sent his secretary in search of a birth certificate for Antonio Hernandez Sanchez, which they said would take ten minutes.

One and a half hours later, we were still waiting, when the director entered. "Senorita Koons, we have checked all our records and called over to Tijuana. There is absolutely no record of Antonio's birth. It's clear that his mother never registered him; it isn't uncommon among poorer Mexicans."

It was amazing that these officials had nothing to offer me. "Can you suggest some other document we could use in place of a birth certificate? Can we use the court papers?"

"No. If he had been placed in an orphanage they would have given him a certificate of abandonment, but La Granja doesn't bother to secure proper documents for the boys."

That was no surprise to me. They didn't do anything right at La Granja. I could have started in about the prison director, but it wouldn't have done any good. "Why don't you just issue him a certificate of abandonment right now?"

"I can't do that, senorita. You don't understand. It's not that easy."

He was so right, I didn't understand. "Well, please tell me, just what can I do?"

"Honestly, I don't know. You could try to persuade that director at the passport office to do something about it, but it would probably be a waste of time. Legally, there's only one solution."

It was hard to believe that there was a solution at all and that he hadn't told us about it already. Eagerly, I urged him on.

"In order to immigrate your adopted son into the United States without a passport, you will have to live with him in Mexico for two and a half years!"

I was too shocked to respond. School starts in a few weeks, I thought. I have classes to prepare for and a million other things demand my attention at home. I've got to get out of this insane office and get home! His idea was impossible, and I wanted to tell him what I thought of it. Instead, Alva and I each took Antonio by an arm and walked him to the car. He seemed very weak.

We had just taken a giant step backward in securing Antonio a birth certificate. It was late afternoon, which meant that we had to go back to the Hotel Lucerna and start over tomorrow. The car was dying fast, but I urged it gently forward. "I think we might have some major car trouble, Alva. Listen to the poor thing." As the knocking sound grew louder and more strained, I pulled to the side of the road.

"Oh, no, I'm too exhausted to even think about fixing the

car. We'll take care of the car tomorrow. If we could only get back to the hotel," I groaned.

"Maybe something cold to drink and a bite to eat would clear our minds, and we could think of a solution. Look, there's a little cafe across the street. Let's go over there."

The air-conditioned restaurant was a welcome relief. "I should have told that man that I've already lived in Mexico for two and a half years. Doesn't it seem that long to you? Now we need to do something about my car, but where can we take it? What would I say to a garage attendant anyway—'Please fixo *mi coche?*' If only David were here!"

Alva nodded toward the waiter. "Why don't we try to talk to him about it?"

That sounded good to me, so Alva and I did our best, using Spanish, English, sign language, and noises to explain our trouble to the waiter. Antonio seemed a little embarrassed at our charades; then it dawned on me that he spoke Spanish.

"Antonio, please, please tell the man about our car. Just tell him that it's broken and ask him what to do."

Poor Antonio, I had heard him say only a few words in all the time I had known him, and now I expected him to explain the mechanical difficulties of our car to a stranger—and all this while feverish.

But before long he was stuttering away in Spanish, making animated gestures with his body to clarify and emphasize his jumbled speech. He kept saying over and over again, "Bumba, bumba, bumba."

Whatever that meant, it was clear to the waiter. "Oh, *si!*" he said, and disappeared into the kitchen.

Within a few minutes a thirty-year-old man wearing grease-streaked clothes walked in, greeted the waiter, and approached our table. In broken English, he explained that he was a mechanic—a relative of the waiter—with a shop a few blocks away.

"Senorita, if you will trust me, I will fix your car in a few hours."

Too tired and too concerned about Antonio to consider an alternative, I gave my consent.

"Carolyn," Alva spoke softly, "Look out the window!" The hood of my car was up, and four men were inspecting the engine. The mechanic went out to join them. I imagined that this could cost me dearly, but I didn't have any choice.

A short time later, Alva was nudging me again. This time my car was being pulled away by a truck that didn't look as though it could pull its own weight. "Good-bye car; by God's grace alone, I'll see you again."

Unable to stall any longer, we braved the heat and jammed ourselves into the mechanic's truck for a ride back to the hotel. As I watched him drive away down the smoldering street, I wondered if we would ever see him or the car again. But I was too tired to care.

Never in my life had I been so tired. Our cool room was like an oasis. I showered in the hope of regaining some composure and cooling my body down. By sheer will power I forced myself to think only of the present until a good night's rest could restore my ability to reason. Antonio and Alva were drained, too. But as we worked together redressing his foot, I marveled at his intense enjoyment of our attention, even though his foot hurt terribly.

We had no trouble getting Antonio to keep his foot up; he was glued to the Mexican cartoons on the black-and-white television set. Lying there on the queen-sized bed, he looked like a little prince. Though Alva and I tried to hide our discouragement, Antonio remained subdued, perhaps actually frightened. How comforting—for both of us—it would have been to talk to him. Spanish words had stuck in my mind amazingly well these past few days, but I was nowhere near able to carry on a conversation with my own son.

The staff at the Hotel Lucerna, having learned of our plight, treated us royally. Several seemed touched by the brave little boy someone cared for enough to go to so much trouble.

As we concluded our meal in the dining room, three Mexican gentleman seated themselves at our table, concerned to see us back at the hotel and to hear of our troubles—word travels fast!

"We understand, senorita, that you cannot get the required papers to get Antonio across the border."

"That's right, we tried everything we could think of for two days—dead ends at every turn."

"Senorita, may we present our solution? It would be very easy for us to get him across the border."

After a day like the one we'd just had, I knew his statement had to have a catch in it. Alva nudged a warning under the table as I asked, "What do you have in mind?"

One of the men leaned forward and lowered his voice to a whisper, "All you have to do is give Antonio to us. Wait about an hour, then drive across the border. We'll be waiting for you at the Foster's Freeze." He glanced at his two friends, and they nodded in agreement, smiling broadly at their splendid idea to bring relief to us.

They meant what they said, and, what's more, they probably could have pulled it off. What a relief it would be to have Antonio across the border. "Thanks, it sounds like a great plan, but I can't do it. Truly, we appreciate your willingness to help, but God has worked a miracle in our lives and we can't cheat now just to hurry things up."

Although surprised at my response, they seemed to respect the faith and courage that lay behind it. If only they knew how fine was the thread of faith that kept me from accepting their offer. Verbalizing my commitment gave me courage: I really *would* rather fail altogether than live with a cheap victory!

We hurried back to our room to get Tony off his swollen foot. Alva and I fell, spent, onto our beds. One fearful, doubting question after another bombarded me. Had I deliberately chosen failure by turning down the Mexican men's offer? Surely that wasn't God's answer? With my last ounce of strength I shook off the sparks of defeat from my volatile weakness.

A knock on the door broke the silence of the night. It was the mechanic! With the smile of a conquering soldier on his face, he held up our car keys. He had repaired the car. I could finally rest a little.

The next morning, I wasted my strength retracing my steps of the day before. The only solution anyone could give me was to live in Mexico for two and a half years. Sometime before noon, I crawled despondently into my car, burning my arms and hands on its interior. I was breathing through my mouth and dripping gallons of perspiration; dehydration seemed like a real possibility. It was hard to care; never had I felt so hot and miserable. Perhaps someone had called the hotel with a solution in my absence. With that glimmer of hope, I managed to get back.

Antonio was on my bed watching television when I walked into the room. "Anybody call?" I asked Alva.

"No. Did you have any luck?"

A shake of my head as I slipped out of my shoes answered her. My spirit seemed to break as I realized that my last efforts had produced absolutely nothing and that a miraculous phone call hadn't come, either. But Antonio was glad to see me and snuggled close as if to cheer me up.

Alva and I talked back and forth for a bit, groping for a plan, or at least a next step. But before long we fell into a hopeless silence. A mountain of disappointment and fatigue became a solid wall of depression that I couldn't see over or get around. The death of my dreams was much more painful than I could have imagined. Failure, ugly defeat, smothered my hopes. A loneliness settled over me such as I've never known. Maybe they were right and getting Antonio out was impossible, but the thought of giving up my job and living in Mexico was intolerable. Should I hide Antonio in the village again and go home without him? What if he disappeared? What's the solution? "God, I feel so confused and exhausted, who can help me?"

Just then I sat bolt upright on the bed, fumbled for my address book, and dialed Lupe's number.

"Who are you calling?" Alva asked, startled from her reading. We both knew that God was our only answer, and I couldn't be calling Him.

"Lupe."

"Why are you calling her? She's in Mexico City." She knew how desperate I had become.

"I don't know," I said, as I frantically ran my hand through my hair, "but I have to call her right now!" With the first ring I hoped she would answer; with the second ring, I chided myself for trying; on the third ring, mocking doubts stung my pride and I sat in despair through the fourth ring; by the fifth, I began to hang up. Just in time, I heard a cheery hello and jerked the receiver back to my ear.

"Lupe—hello Lupe, is that you?"

"Yes, this is Lupe. Is that you, Carolyn?"

"Yes, Lupe. What are you doing in the office? We thought you were in Mexico City." I practically yelled into the phone.

Lupe laughed. "I know, but there was so much work to do that I postponed my trip until today. My flight leaves in a few minutes; in fact, I was on my way out to catch the plane and just dropped by the office to check my mail. The door's still wide open. What about you?" she inquired. "Does Antonio like his new home?"

"I don't know. We're still in Mexicali. We can't get out of Mexico without a birth certificate for Antonio, and we don't have one. Lupe, is there anything at all you can do?"

She didn't hesitate for a moment. "Come over to the office right away. I'll cancel my flight."

I could hardly contain myself. God *did* have his hand on us—to think there had been such a brief few minutes in which Lupe could have been reached. We set a record for fast packing and departure.

Lupe greeted us with hugs and kisses and smothered Antonio with attention once again. He was visibly relieved to be with her.

Lupe listened with sober attention to a blow-by-blow account of our four days' journey since we'd last seen her. When I had finished, she stared out the window, digesting what I'd told her. When she turned back, it was to say, "Carolyn, they are absolutely right. Without a birth certificate or a passport, the law requires you to live in Mexico with Antonio for two and a half years."

Chapter Thirteen

Nightmares sometimes seem very real. Perhaps I'd awaken soon and find that this whole mess with the passport had been a bad dream.

But no, the wicked edict stood firm; there were two options, and whichever I chose would drastically change my life. Lupe and Alva were quiet, and I was carried off into my imagination. Back at home, I was packing up my house, saying good-bye to my students and friends at the university, arranging to cash in my retirement fund or an investment so that I could live in Mexico with my son. Then, after thirty long months, we would move back to the United States—legally.

"Legally." I said it aloud and jerked myself into the present. "Lupe, this is so incongruous. How can they illegally imprison a child and then rigidly enforce a passport regulation? Everyone around here functions like an underprogrammed computer."

"You can't be blamed for being bitter, Carolyn."

"I'm not bitter," I interrupted, "I'm angry! There's got to be a weak link in this law somewhere, Lupe. Think!"

"Sure, just get a signature from the governor of the state. Unfortunately, he doesn't do things like that!"

"This is tearing me apart. I can't leave my home, my job, and my country just because Antonio's mother neglected to register his birth. There seems to be a conspiracy against Antonio. Neglected, blamed for murder, imprisoned, sold—and now cheated out of his only chance of happiness." Near tears, I fell silent. Antonio was standing at my side, and I hugged him close.

Abruptly, Lupe stood up and paced around the room, apparently mulling something over. "Carolyn, I have an idea; it's a long shot, but we don't have anything to lose."

"What's your long shot, Lupe? I'm ready to try anything!"

"About three months ago, I attended a major conference in Mexico City for officials from all the various states. One day I was invited out to lunch by, would you believe, the governor's personal executive secretary." Growing excitement enlivened her voice. "During the meal she asked me to tell her about any exciting cases I was working on. Well, nothing's been more exciting and involved than your case with Antonio, so I gave her a detailed account. She was interested that someone like you would become so involved with a little Mexican prisoner. As we parted, she asked me to keep her informed."

"Let's not disappoint her, Lupe! Keep her informed right now!" I gestured toward the telephone.

Lupe dialed the governor's office. I all but broke out in cold chills. She winked at me, and we laughed at our boldness. "I'll give it my best, Carolyn, but it'll be a miracle if they even put our call through."

She broke off and began a conversation in Spanish with someone on the phone. There was a deadly pause, then she began speaking again. I could understand just enough Spanish to know that she had gotten through and was talking with the governor's secretary. Antonio's eyes were wide with interest, since he understood every word she was saying. Alva and I strained just to catch the gist of the conversaion.

Finally, when the tension seemed unbearable, Lupe made an okay sign with her fingers. Sharply, she hung up the phone and grabbed her attaché case and purse. "Let's go! Senora Romero will see us if we can get there before lunch." Lupe teased Antonio by pinching his cheek. "The idea of seeing Antonio thrilled her."

Spurred by new hope, we raced across town, hardly noticing that it had reached 115 degrees outside. How good it was to go past the third-floor passport office directly to the reception area of the governor's suite. With a strange mixture of sweet, grandmotherly assurance and executive finesse, Senora Romero reached for Antonio and enfolded him in her arms. Although impeccably dressed and dripping with sophistication, she evoked a response from Antonio that a beloved grandmother might have received. I could have fainted when she hugged Alva, Lupe, and me as well!

Ushering us into her sumptuous-looking office, she asked Lupe for the papers. Both of us responded, eagerly handing her packets of documents. She laughed; then, with fine-tuned concentration, she examined our documents and announced, "Splendid, everything is here!" Satisfied, she gathered the papers to her bosom and disappeared through a beautifully carved, twelve-foot oak door into the inner domain of the state's governor.

Nervously rubbing my hands up and down the fine soft leather of the chair, I passed the agonizing wait admiring the elegantly furnished office. Polished marble floors in the foyer contrasted nicely with the posh gold of the office carpet. An exquisite antique clock and oil paintings depicting dignitaries of years past were displayed against rich oak paneling. The high ceiling dwarfed the massive furniture. An hour ago our troubles had been so bad I could hardly believe it; now things were too good to be true. Antonio sat enchanted.

Fifteen minutes passed before Senora Romero emerged from the governor's office, and I held my breath as she handed me a document and pointed to the bottom of the page. There it was, the governor's signature. Before anyone could respond, she was marching toward the door. "Follow me!" she commanded like a general. I was at a semi-run trying to keep up with her rapid pace and thought how much like a clutch of chickens we must have looked. Through long corridors and down two flights of stairs we went to make our grand entrance at the door of the crowded passport office. The instant the director and his assistants caught sight of the governor's secretary and her entourage, they snapped to attention. Senora Romero pushed the document toward the director and waited as he read down the page. He gasped as he saw the governor's signature.

"It will only take a few moments, senora, to prepare this passport," the director said respectfully. Then he turned to me, "Do you still have Antonio's passport pictures?" Triumphantly I handed them to him.

With hugs and kisses around our circle, Senora Romero said that she needed to get back to work. "I hope that one day I will see you again, Antonio. You are very special." She had heard our story only a few months before and just minutes ago become involved, but her genuine concern had produced a miracle. What a wonderful, generous woman. Quietly, I thanked God for her.

The director returned, carrying a stack of passports. "Stop praying, Carolyn," Lupe teased. "We only need one passport." Expectancy charged the room. A ceremony of sorts began as the director read the name on a passport, shook the recipient's hand, and watched each person leave the office. As the stack dwindled, I began to get nervous. Only a few passports remained; the office was very quiet, almost empty. "Oh God, please don't—" I couldn't ask; God already knew! Three to go, two to go . . .

Ceremoniously, the director opened the last passport and looked at Antonio with a huge smile, announcing, "Antonio Koons!" The tension broken, Antonio's little band of tired warriors almost collapsed with relief. But Antonio knew exactly what to do. He had to stand on his tiptoes to see over the counter and reach up to receive his treasured passport. The director's hand reached down to meet Antonio's and he asked, "Antonio Koons?"

"*Si!*" His proud voice rang out clearly.

Looking intently into Antonio's eyes, the director said, "You are a very lucky boy!"

Tears filled Antonio's eyes; he knew that he was lucky, and he dipped his head to wipe his tears on his shirt.

Looking at us over Antonio's head, the director told us in a husky voice, "Senoritas, I have worked in this office for seventeen years and in all that time the governor has never given his personal signature to issue a passport. This truly is a lucky boy!"

We all wiped joyful tears from our eyes and enjoyed Antonio's delight. Somehow, through all the confusion, the meaning of this passport was clear to Antonio—he was going home!

It was nearly noon on Friday, and we huddled to make a decision on our next step. We'd been in Mexico since Monday, and I knew if we didn't cross the border today we couldn't get Antonio processed until next Monday. The thought was intolerable. I just wanted to get out of Mexico, go home, and get acquainted with my new son.

"What do you say we try to make it to the immigration office in Tijuana by five this afternoon, Alva? I would love to get home tonight."

"The sooner the better," Alva agreed. "I'm beginning to feel like a prisoner down here."

Lupe was ecstatic, "Yes, yes, you should go. It's worth the try."

She had been so good about everything; I loved her for canceling her flight and helping us today. We hugged each other one last time and made a mad dash for the car.

"Hop in, Lupe. We'll take you by your office."

"No, no," she urged us on. "It would add thirty minutes to your trip. I'll grab a cab. Good luck, Carolyn. Good luck, Alva. I love you, Antonio!"

He ran to Lupe, wrapped his skinny arms around her body, and gave her a big kiss. It used to be just me, then Antonio and me, but each day our family grew bigger. Lupe was a special part.

Our spirits were high, and I patted the dash. "You're doing great, ol' car, don't give up now." The car must have understood; it hummed beautifully over the mountains. Antonio was too excited to be sick and sat between us tenderly opening and closing his passport. For a long time he studied his photograph; it must have been the first he'd ever seen of himself.

The trip was refreshingly uneventful, and right on schedule we walked into the immigration office. "This is the way I like things to go, Antonio." I talked to him all the time now, just as if he could understand me—and sometimes he did.

It wasn't without commotion that we entered the office and caught the busy Mr. Solomon by surprise. He looked past the other people at us as though he'd seen a ghost and walked out from behind the counter to meet us. His secretary followed.

Showing him Antonio's passport was my only interest, so I handed it to him as he approached. "This should do it, Mr. Solomon," I beamed.

He looked at me incredulously, "My God, I didn't think I'd ever see you again!"

Working hard to keep my voice normal, I said, "That's okay, my God knew that I would be seeing *you!*"

"How did you get this passport?" He seemed unnerved.

Almost in unison, Alva and I answered, "The governor of the state," and I continued, "gave his personal signature for Antonio's release!"

I reminded Mr. Solomon of his promise to process Antonio's papers and grant his visa on the same day we arrived.

"You're right!" he said, "and I'm going to handle this myself." Then he escorted us behind the counter and into his office, along with his secretary. Pushing all the papers on his desk aside, he carefully laid out Antonio's portfolio, then asked his secretary for the papers from Washington, D.C., that they had filed away.

I kept glancing at my watch; it was past four. "Do you think we're going to make it?"

He remained silent an anxious moment, "Miss Koons, you're missing one document! Where is Antonio's medical?"

"Mr. Solomon, no one has ever mentioned anything about a medical! What medical?"

"In order to be granted a visa he needs a physical."

Home was only an elusive dream—something I'd invented in my mind. Really, I was an eternal office tramp without purpose or goal. "Mr. Solomon, we could have had a physical done anytime this week if I'd known."

"I'm sorry, Miss Koons. It's just another oversight, but I can't give you a visa until it's done. You'll have to wait until

Monday, but there shouldn't be any problem at all getting a physical then."

"Why can't somebody do it right now?"

"Sorry again, Miss Koons, the doctor's office is just down the street, but they're only open Monday through Thursday." Mr. Solomon shrugged helplessly.

I felt cursed. "What about a nurse or a technician? Isn't there anyone who could give him a physical? Surely there is a doctor in town who works on Fridays!"

He was deflating. "There's only one doctor in Tijuana certified to give visa medicals."

Blind to reason, I pushed once more: "Please do me a favor and call the doctor's office just to see if there's a chance."

To humor me and soothe my anxiety, Mr. Solomon called the office. Soon he held his hand over the receiver and said, "Guess what, someone just saw Dr. Potter walking through the office complex; if you can locate him, maybe he'll be gracious enough to give Antonio a physical today. But I doubt it, Miss Koons. He's pretty rigid, and besides, no one could find him just now. Why don't you three run down to the office and try to find him?" Quickly he drew us a map.

The afternoon sun was still hot as we ran two full blocks to the medical building. Antonio's foot was, thankfully, much better. Though scribbled, the map was accurate, and we found the building. "Alva, let's separate and run up and down the corridors yelling for Dr. Potter." From our hysteria, everyone must have thought somebody was dying—and I couldn't promise they wouldn't if we didn't get that physical. We were acting so crazy I wondered if they might try to lock us up. Antonio was highly amused at it all.

Antonio and I turned the corner full tilt, yelling for Dr. Potter, and found him talking with another doctor. Of course he listened, what else could he do?

"Oh yes, Miss Koons, Mr. Solomon just told me you were looking for me."

Going on, I told him our situation. "Please, Dr. Potter, we've worked for Antonio's release for years, and this physical is the only thing keeping us from going home. He looked down at Antonio, and before I knew what had happened, we were whisked into the office. God had softened another heart.

At 4:20 P.M., Dr. Potter began to examine Antonio. He thumped him here and there, looked into his eyes, ears, and nose, then said, "Say 'ah.' Good boy, fine." Leaning over the medical form he made quick work of the lengthy question-naire. "He's as healthy as a horse."

We hugged Dr. Potter, and I can't remember if we paid him or not, but his hearty laughter followed us down the corridor and onto the sidewalk. Our crazy trio was at a full run once again, screaming our thanks to the good doctor all the way.

Back at the consulate, Mr. Solomon had, in spite of his doubts, continued processing the papers. They were being typed by three secretaries while he supervised everything. The signed medical form we produced was almost too much for him to believe. Definitely, this was a Mexican revolution of time and efficiency! His whole office and staff and everyone waiting joined our zany rally.

In a flurry of excitement, Mr. Solomon gathered one paper after another and piled them on a stack before me, then crowned his efforts with Antonio's visa. "Now, *I* would like some pictures," he announced. We hurried into family-portrait position, laughing, then flew out the door in a confu-sion of hurried thank-yous and good-byes and promises to let them know how things turned out.

At American Immigration, Alva let us out of the car. "I'll drive across the line and wait for you there. My prayers are with you."

"Okay, Alva, we'll see you in a couple of hours." She blew Antonio a kiss and drove away.

We stepped into the office only minutes before they locked the doors. Another long wait! There were hundreds of people ahead of us, but the procedure was simple. Antonio's visa and passport would be exchanged for the much-coveted green card that would allow him legal entry into the United States.

For the first time since I'd met Antonio, we were alone together, and now he was my son. Strange feelings fluttered around in my stomach.

Our wait was surprisingly short; before we knew it we were crossing the border on a bridge that overlooks Mexico and the United States as well as a river of cars making the crossing. Antonio and I ran down onto the American side both laughing and crying.

Ready with the camera, Alva captured the glory of the moment: Antonio and I standing with our arms wrapped around each other holding up his beautiful green card for all the world to see—Antonio Hernandez Sanchez Koons and his new mom!

Chapter Fourteen

Strong hunger pangs reminded me that our last meal, breakfast, had been twelve hours earlier. Was it humanly possible to accomplish all we had today? Excesses of disappointment, hope, defeat, and victory, had made this one of the most exciting days of my life. A little hum of contentment soothed my aching body as I felt my son's warmth against my side on the drive back to Los Angeles.

Antonio looked the picture of contentment himself, sitting between his new mom and new grandma. For twelve years he had wrestled with mounting injustice to gain his freedom, and this very hour he'd been released to begin his new life. I was very proud of him, he was a fighter and the victory belonged to him.

The mystery of Antonio's whereabouts for the last nine months had not yet been solved, but somewhere, sometime, he had been exposed to advertising, probably on television. As we drove along he pointed to various billboards and pronounced the words, "Coke, McDonald's, Chevy, Texaco, and tequila." Alva and I enjoyed it immensely. He was really warming up.

The McDonald's billboards especially excited him, so I turned into the first McDonald's restaurant that we found.

"May I take your order?" the waitress asked through the speaker box at the drive-through.

Antonio nearly jumped out of his skin at the strange box. He laughed and pointed at it as we continued up to the window. By the time I finished placing our order for hamburgers and cokes he had pretty well figured out the procedure for ordering. Antonio devoured his hamburger, relieving my concern about his poor appetite of the last few days.

From McDonald's we went to the bus station. Grandma

Alva needed to get home to her family, but it was very hard to explain to Antonio that she was going to her faraway home and that we wouldn't be seeing her for a while. Grandma Alva knew how to make Antonio feel cared for, and their relationship had blossomed over the past week. Words could never express to Alva my gratitude for the support she had given to both Antonio and me. It was hard to see her go.

I knew it was time for me to seriously face motherhood. So far, I didn't feel any different. I've always loved children —especially older children that I can work with and teach new and exciting things to. And I loved Antonio. What would he have been like as a baby, or even at nine years old when I first found him, instead of twelve? Oh well, there would be plenty of time to get to know him.

He sat quietly beside me, and I said, "Grandma Alva?" Antonio nodded and remained quiet. I knew he was thinking about her. We would see her again in just a week, and I patted his knee. "We're going home, son."

Our day narrowed down to one last but very important task; I was about to introduce him to his new home—the house in which we would work and play and grow together.

So many times I had come alone down this winding little road toward home, never dreaming that one day I would be bringing a twelve-year-old son with me.

"Antonio, press this button, it will open the garage door." With the remote control on his lap, I pushed the button. Like an excited pup, Antonio went into action and all but wagged his tail. While the engine was still running, he jumped out of the car and began exploring the garage. "Hey, tiger, let's go inside." He reached out for his suitcase and bounded ahead of me. Ducking in and out of each room he ran all over the house, up and down the stairs and through the whole house again. As he came down the stairs again I caught him in my arms. "Antonio, let me show you our home!" It was fun to point out various things that I knew would thrill him, like the color television set and a giant refrigerator-freezer with honest to goodness ice cream.

Antonio and I laughed together in sheer delight as we moved from room to room. Upstairs in my room, I suggested, "Antonio, sit on the bed." He sat down, slush, slush, and shot off the bed in horror. Incredulity froze his face as he felt the bed curiously. In short order I stripped the sheets back and explained my waterbed to him. Antonio readily accepted everything with an adventurous spirit.

Together we walked outside onto the balcony and looked down at the pool shimmering in the moonlight. The peace it reflected contrasted sharply with the turmoil that we had left in Mexico. So we stood quietly a few moments before I nudged him to continue our tour.

"This is your room, Antonio," I explained, showing him the room next to mine.

"For me?" he finally said, tenderly touching the big double bed and dresser where he would keep his very own things. It was shockingly different from the room he had shared with two hundred and fifty other boys. His eyes filled with tears of happiness, and he sat there in his new room for the longest time, just looking and touching each piece of furniture.

Earlier in the day I had phoned Don and Pauline Grant and given them the good news that we were on our way home, so when the doorbell rang I wasn't surprised to see them and their children. They brought dessert and a party spirit to meet my new son, and we praised God together for his goodness. David and Sue came and were next to join the party. They had been wondering where we had disappeared to that week after sending them home on the bus. It wasn't without tears that we celebrated that night.

Everyone pretended not to notice Antonio moving curiously from one new thing to another. He didn't just look at things, he carefully studied them.

Seeing Antonio settled in his new bed that night, I hoped the old iron bed at La Granja could rapidly be forgotten. We prayed simply and thanked God for a new beginning. "Good night, Antonio. Sleep well," I said and kissed his head.

"Good night, Mama." I smiled at how good that strange new word made me feel.

Gloriously I fell into my own bed, too tired to think of the past and too scared to think of the future. For now I would be content to take one day at a time. Anyway, if being a mother meant going through weeks like this one, I'd better get some sleep.

Chapter Fifteen

There is something terribly shocking about instant parenting: one minute you're free as a bird, the next, you're definitely not. And it's so permanent—twenty-four hours a day, forever (or so it seems). As these thoughts soaked through the warmth of my optimism to the chilling reality of making myself do things I didn't want to do at all, I talked to God. "We really need your help, Lord. Antonio doesn't know how to be a son and I sure don't know how to be a mother. This first year is going to be very rough, considering all the adjustments we have to make. Lord, I'm going to commit this first year completely to Antonio—no speaking, no traveling, unless he comes with me—he's going to be number one."

It would be tough, but I felt prepared for anything, and after all, a year wasn't forever. By the second year we would both be old hands at this family thing, and I could resume my regular lifestyle for the most part.

The first week Antonio was home was something like an arranged marriage. I knew nothing of his world, and he knew nothing of mine. Yet we had to integrate our individualities into one new and very different way of living.

Whereas most parents have their children over a lifetime and see gradual changes and growth, with Antonio I saw huge changes from hour to hour. He was fascinating just to watch, as every minute was filled with new discoveries and wonderful adventures. Letting him out of my sight for too long proved to be a mistake, though. I showed him how to turn on the faucets so he could wash his hands but then went on with my own work. I discovered shortly that he had dismantled the faucet to discover how it worked. The only problem was that he couldn't put it back together, so I rolled up my sleeves and took over. But while I did that, he discovered the kitchen lamp and took it apart. Hiding my tools became a necessity, but I did encourage Antonio to study how things worked without taking them apart. It was amazing to see how much Antonio didn't know; our home and garage held all the thrill of a Disneyland.

Our communication problems were minimal, considering that each of us spoke a language foreign to the other. Antonio was quickly picking up English, and David and Sue dropped by frequently that first week and explained things to him. Antonio and I became very good at sign language as well.

One afternoon, David said, "Antonio, we have a little problem here. Either you're going to have to learn English or your mom needs to learn Spanish. Which do you think we should do?"

"English! I think I better learn English!" he stated to David—in Spanish.

"And maybe you'd like an American name," I suggested. "Shall we call you Antonio Koons, or would you prefer Anthony or Tony?"

He didn't understand at once, but when he did, he was delighted. "Tony," he said. "*Me llamo Tony.*"

Most of the things Tony did amused me. However, his addiction to the music on our radio was most unsettling. When he walked in the room he either brought a radio with him or turned one on—very loud. Even though I hated the intrusion of blaring music, gradual weaning was necessary from a habit so well ingrained. At La Granja, the minute our Outreach teams walked out the door loud radio music was switched on in the dorm, hyping the boys into a near frenzy. Tony clung to the radio as a pacifier.

Encouragement and praise were as new to Tony as calculators and waterbeds, so I made it a point to compliment him frequently and encourage even his slightest efforts with generous praise. It was fun to watch his little chest swell with pride.

During that first week I also noticed how difficult it was for Tony to change pace and move from one activity to the next.

Perhaps this was due to the institutional environment to which he was accustomed. If nothing else, prison life was predictable. Too many choices or a lack of structure overwhelmed him to the point that he couldn't function.

Quickly I made up a schedule for meals, bedtime, and some activities that would contribute to his sense of well-being. This was very hard for me. I always made it to work and appointments on time, but as a single person I never set a schedule for eating. Sometimes I didn't bother to eat at all, or I would go to a restaurant or to a friend's house. Freedom was the mark of my singleness and I thrived on change and variety.

But more difficult than having scheduled meals was planning the menus and preparing the food. Before Tony, I always ate my main meal at the university or at a restaurant; everything else was strictly a snack. Perhaps I was going to learn as much as Tony, or maybe even more.

Tony's eating habits were interesting, too. His favorites were the all-American hamburgers, hot dogs, and pizza. Mexican meals were also high on his list. Tony would walk into the kitchen at dinner time and sniff around, "What are you doing, Mom?"

"I'm cooking tacos for dinner, Tony."

"They don't fix them that way in Mexico!"

"Why don't you show me how they cook tacos in Mexico? I would love to learn." It was an insulting suggestion at best, judging from the response he gave me.

"Mexican men don't cook. Only the women work in the kitchen." He stomped out of the kitchen and rarely returned to visit with me while I prepared our meals. Oh well, that would come later. After all, I wasn't much used to cooking, either! Whether my cooking was authentic Mexican or not, Tony continued to eat like tomorrow would never come. But he was still very skinny and needed the extra calories.

I kept Tony's wardrobe quite basic. The new clothing that we bought him in Mexicali was extravagant to him compared with what he had worn in the prison. Actually, it would have been fun to dress him handsomely—he was so cute—but it would have been a poor idea. Just the clothing he had overwhelmed him. His concept of clothing was to wear a garment until it fell off his body, I guess. Each morning, he put on exactly what he'd worn the day before and couldn't understand the concept of alternating outfits while the dirty clothing was being washed. If he felt comfortable, that's all that mattered to Tony, and the ritual of "clean clothes" was an inconvenience.

If we planned to go out and I suggested to him that he change his clothes and get cleaned up, he became totally frustrated. What seemed like a simple request to me ruined Tony's composure and sometimes our whole evening. After a few tries I dropped this subject with him and gathered his dirty clothes after he was asleep. There were so many things for him to learn, relearn, and unlearn that I chose not to make an issue of what he wore or didn't wear.

The less change Tony had in his life the more secure and happy he felt. This was very difficult for me; I love change.

One day during the first week I suggested to Antonio that he play with his cars, since there were a lot of chores for me to do. Compliantly he went up to his room while I worked. Several times I stuck my head in and observed him lying on the floor playing very intently with his little match-box cars. He was so involved with his imaginary world that he didn't even notice me at the door. At lunch time I called him to come and eat, and when he didn't respond I went up to check on him.

"Tony, come down and have some lunch?"

"No, I want to play."

"Wouldn't you like just a sandwich?"

"No."

"Would you like some fruit or milk?"

"No."

So I went on with my chores but later took his sandwich to him on a paper plate. The sandwich sat there all afternoon while Tony completely lost himself in the world of little cars

and trucks. Finally, at dinner time I bribed him to the table
with his favorite taco dinner, but not without gentle motherly
encouragement all the way from his bedroom to the table.

At times during the day I almost forgot Tony was in the
house. He was in his room an awfully long time. He had spent
six hours in concentrated child's play, and again I realized that
Tony was making up for lost time—cramming his stolen childhood years into days. I knew that he would have to play many
more quiet hours to regain the years he had lost. It felt really
good to begin to understand my child's needs.

Dinner time was most enjoyable. As we ate, we conversed
in our own animated, simple language. My hand was resting
on the table and Tony reached across and touched it gently.
It was good to feel my son reach out to me and begin to see
our relationship grow. Looking down at our hands I noticed
that Tony's index and middle fingers were badly scarred from
burns. I ached to really talk with him and ask him about his
fingers, his feelings, what he was thinking, and maybe even
about his mother. But for now the only thing I could do was
squeeze his hand and wait patiently. My stack of questions
about Tony grew hourly. It was hard not to wonder what was
going on behind his big brown eyes.

One night I was awakened by terrifying screams. I quickly
flipped on the light and ran to Tony's room to find him struggling in the grip of an awful nightmare. "Don't hit me, don't
hit me," he screamed in English. I drew his sweat-drenched
body close and rocked him gently until his sobs subsided. Poor
Tony. His scars were much more than fingertip deep. How
many times had he been beaten? Counselor friends assured me
that nightmares were only natural for one who had had such
a childhood. But just how deep did these wounds penetrate
his spirit? Would he ever wake up at night to a sense of
security? Startled into consciousness, would he always find
himself in La Granja? "Oh God," I prayed, "help Tony turn
the past loose and live for now."

Those first four weeks with Tony were fun. I became so
lost in the wonder of his new world that the world outside our

Chapel time in Mexico, with our canvas village in the background.

Our first view of La Granja. I grew to hate this fence that imprisoned the boys.

That first day inside the prison. We were fascinated by Antonio's sparkling eyes.

One filthy toilet for 250 boys.

One slimy urinal . . .

We spent as many hours as we could visiting Antonio at the prison that first week.

Many of the boys were confined for months in the dorm.

The steel door that
secured the boys' dorm.

Two and a half years
after our first meeting.
My first day of mother-
hood . . . becoming a
nurse.

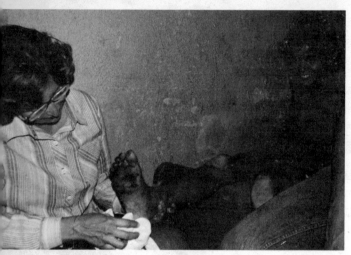

A team member gives Antonio assurance after the
beating incident. "You'd better get him out of here
before they kill him," Armando urged.

Amelia, Antonio, and I stealing
moments together on our first return
trip to the prison.

Our visit to La Granja one year later. Bright-eyed Antonio had no idea that Pastor Peters would eventually become Grandpa.

Closed doors! We couldn't get out of Mexico. Moments later I called Lupe . . . our last hope.

Marvelous Lupe Puga, our lawyer.

Antonio ate *everything* on the table at his first birthday party.

Antonio shaking hands with Mr. Solomon, Director of Immigration in Tijuana.

After his first, *long* shower Antonio, sporting his new clothes and ready for dinner, beamed.

After one month in the United States, Tony was thrilled with all the newness of his world.

Tony's surprise graduation speech. It made it all worthwhile.

Tony's eighth-grade graduation picture. He's the cutest kid in the class!

The would-be soccer champ.

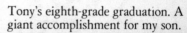

Tony's eighth-grade graduation. A giant accomplishment for my son.

Tony's twelfth-grade graduation. Thank you, Lord!

four walls dimmed for the first time in my life. I couldn't believe that I had been in my house almost constantly for weeks. I had always left my house at least once a day, even if it was only to go for a drive. But Tony liked being in the house —all day, every day. That commitment I'd made to God made it much easier. For one year I could take anything.

The highlight of Tony's week was a television program about the "Bionic Man," whose superhuman strength enabled him to twist steel with his hands, jump to the tops of tall buildings, and see over incredible distances. Soon the "Bionic Mom" game developed at our house. I simply turned into a woman of awesome powers and stalked after my giggling son making gruesome sounds. He loved to be roughed up and tickled and hugged and scared to death by his fierce mama. We called this our goof-off time and it was precious therapy for both of us. Nearly every night he signaled me by saying, "goof-off time, Mom!" We laughed until our sides ached.

"If only my students could see me now," I sometimes mused. Would they be shocked to know that I stayed home these days and played monster games?

After a few weeks of getting acquainted, I decided it was safe to venture out into the world. So we packed our things and made the seven-hour drive to visit Grandma Alva and Grandpa Russell. It was a great break for me, and Tony enjoyed seeing his grandma and meeting her family and friends. I noticed that people just sat back and watched Tony; he was so caught up with the newness of life.

The first few weeks had gone so well that I began to wonder if we'd need a whole year for our adjustments. This mothering business wasn't so bad after all. I thought that someone should give me a little pat on the back.

Our visit to Tony's grandparents had been so successful that I decided to accept an invitation from the Grant family to visit them at their beachside condominium. Tony hadn't yet seen the ocean. He was awed by the magnitude of the Pacific but we were unable to persuade him to go in any further than ankle deep. Probably he couldn't swim. He wouldn't go near

the pool at home; he said there were "too many people."
More exciting than the beach, though, was the Grants' little
dog, Burp. Burp and Tony were instant and inseparable
friends.

After a beautiful day on the beach, we all decided to go
out for dinner—a real treat for me after staying so close to
home for so long. Because the group was large and not everyone was prepared to spend a great deal, we decided to choose
one of the two moderately priced specials, either chicken or
steak. Carefully, I explained the plan to Tony and waited for
him to choose.

But pictured on the front of the menu was the most expensive item listed, steak and lobster. It was more than double the
price of the other choices. Tony eyed it for some time, then
pointed to it and said, "I want this one!" Everyone laughed
nervously.

"No, I'm sorry, Tony, tonight you need to choose one of
these," and I pointed out his choices. "That's what we're all
doing tonight."

Tony's expression became more determined. This time, he
said, *"No,* I want this one!" and pointed at the steak and
lobster.

The other children tittered, and Don Grant said, "Okay,
Mom, how are you going to handle this one?" I had figured
on some clashes, but, for goodness' sakes, not in front of all
these people!

Gently, I said, "Tony, all these people"—I pointed to each
one seated around our table—"are going to choose one of
these, and so are you."

Now Tony was belligerent. He brought his fist down on
the picture and said, "I want this one!"

Everyone's ears perked up and all conversation dropped
off. The war was on, and as far as I was concerned, the world
was watching.

To my relief, our cheerful waiter approached. At least for
a few minutes, the spotlight would be off Tony and me. He
proceeded to take orders around the table, eventually coming

to Tony. "And what will you have, young man?"

Tony glanced toward me with fiery defiance in his eyes. (Could this be the same boy I'd been living with the past few weeks? Maybe I'd picked up the wrong kid on the beach.) Once again he pointed to the steak and lobster. And, once again, very gently, I asked, "Do you want steak, or chicken?" He silently pointed to the picture.

You lose, young man, I thought to myself and, looking up at the waiter, I shrugged, "My son isn't eating tonight, thank you."

Tony looked as though he had just been slapped across the face. He couldn't believe I would do this to him.

The waiter pressed: "Are you sure, madam? Are you sure he wouldn't like to eat?" Tony, a real die-hard, boldly pointed to the picture again.

"I'm sure. He doesn't want anything, but I'd love the steak, please."

We all got up and went to the salad bar, leaving Tony by himself. It was hard to do—very hard—but if he controlled me tonight, where would it end?

I lingered at the salad bar, a bit confused, but several of the Grants complimented me on my decision. When I went back to our table I could see the hurt look on Tony's face. During dinner, Don and his son Glen passed Tony pieces of bread under the table. I would have had to be blind not to notice, but I pretended I hadn't. The remainder of our dinner was enjoyably spent, chatting and visiting for quite a long time.

Back at the condominium, I asked Tony to go for a walk with me. "Well, son, it was pretty bad in the restaurant, wasn't it?"

Tony scuffed his feet. "Yes."

"It was bad for me too, Tony. I tried desperately to save us both embarrassment by reasoning with you." He seemed to soften. "Tony, I love you very much, but don't ever do that again. You came off as the most spoiled and obnoxious kid!"

"But, Mom," Tony argued, "I didn't know the menu."

"Son, you didn't *need* to know the menu; your two choices were very clear." I watched his head drop contritely and realized that he was through fighting. He accepted the comfort of my arm around his shoulder.

"Come on, let's go back. We'll fix you a sandwich." Our first confrontation ended, we headed back to the Grants'. After I made the sandwich, we joined the group for a good movie on television.

At eleven, Don announced it was time to hit the sack. It'd been a long day and we were all tired. I began pulling out the bed for Tony and told him to turn the television off. He changed the channel instead. "Oh, Mom, look! I love this show." It was another of his favorites, cops and robbers. I stood and watched it with him for a few minutes, then turned it off.

Tony's metamorphosis was so quick that it shocked me. He defiantly turned the television back on again. I turned it off, and just as quickly, he turned it back on again. The prison director was right; Tony *didn't* give in easily. Coaxing, reasoning, insisting—nothing reached him. We didn't get to bed until one that morning, but he didn't watch the program. Even so, I felt more tired than victorious. The next morning Tony was back to normal, enjoying Burp and everyone.

The summer was nearly over, and Tony was settling in with more grace than I had dared anticipate. He was picking up English rapidly, which solved our communication problem, at least for the everyday aspects of life.

One afternoon I got a call from a friend at the university inviting me to a "boy shower." I felt awkward at the thought of receiving gifts—not something I had much practice in—but at the same time it sounded fun for Tony. I considered it a gesture of encouragement and accepted.

It was exciting to watch Tony open his gifts. Instead of diapers and baby blankets, he received a wallet, clothing (including a jacket), some model airplanes, more small cars, and to top it off, a watch and a soccer ball. Tony's delight made the evening a real success. As the evening wore on, a note of parental confidence began to surface within me.

The room was crowded with many friends I hadn't seen for almost two months, and we stood around chatting about everything under the sun. "Carolyn!" someone spoke, and everyone's attention seemed to turn on me. Tony was on the floor busily making roads in the deep carpet with his shiny new cars. I turned to find the face that belonged to the voice. "Carolyn," the woman's strident voice continued, "You'll never make it. I give you less than a year and I'll bet you dump him!" Stifled gasps constricted into an embarrassed silence. I tried to shrug off her thoughtless and cruel comment, but the stinger had lodged deep.

How could she say such a thing, I thought to myself. Tony is my son. My hurt turned to anger. I'll show her! Little did I know then how those words would haunt me in the months to come.

Chapter Sixteen

Hot August melted into the still-rising temperatures of September, and making a decision about where to enroll Tony in school couldn't be delayed. He still took things apart and made new discoveries about his world each day, and his progress at speaking English was a marvel. In very basic terms, I would explain the meaning of a word he didn't understand, and it would automatically become part of his vocabulary. He delighted in learning new words and rarely forgot their meanings. When our friends talked over his head, I would realize that he was watching me for an interpretation and repeat the sentence in simple terms. I loved to hear him use new words and complimented him generously.

Several professional counselors warned me, "Carolyn, don't expect too much from Tony. He's been abused and deprived and has lived like an animal most of his life." So I tried to keep my expectations reasonable, but at the same time I wanted him to reach his full potential. Sometimes I even caught myself forgetting his past and treating him as though he had always been mine. It was hard to keep the proper balance.

At La Granja, Tony could have chosen classroom instruction for two hours a week, taught by some volunteers from a local junior college, but he hadn't. So at age twelve he'd had no education. In fact, he couldn't so much as write his own name. Boys his age were now entering the seventh grade, so I thought about starting at least in the sixth grade—he was small anyway. But the sixth graders knew a lot. No matter where we started him, he would be lost academically. We surely couldn't put him in kindergarden! So fifth grade it was.

Busing him to a bilingual school was one possibility, but English wasn't his problem. Tony wanted friends desperately, and busing would take him out of our neighborhood all the way over to another town. There was a park and elementary school just two blocks from our home. There, he would be with children from our church and neighborhood and be more likely to make friends.

Tony had received a hand-me-down bike from the Grants. On our Mexicali Outreach trip I remembered seeing decorated bikes ridden by some of the Mexican children. Bikes were their prized possessions, and Tony was no exception. He loved it! He frequently rode to the school or park and watched the kids but couldn't seem to make friends. He still stuttered badly; perhaps that was a barrier.

Of the many possibilities for Tony's education, all posed problems because he was such an exception, but I finally chose the school nearest our house; it would be easier for him to make friends and for me to be accessible to his teachers.

The principal, Mr. Edwards, was enthusiastic about Tony coming to his school. "I'm sure he'll get along fine, Carolyn. We'll really work with him. We have three sixth-grade classes, two taught by women and one taught by a man, Mr. Bradley. His class is a fifth- and sixth-grade combination, and he is also one of our favorite teachers. I suggest we enroll Tony in Mr. Bradley's class as a fifth grader and look toward moving him into the sixth grade next semester. I think the male image will be good for Tony because that's what he's used to."

Mr. Edwards's suggestion sounded wise, and the interest he took in Tony pleased me. The fifth/sixth-grade class seemed the perfect solution.

"We'll need to find a solution for Tony's reading problem, Carolyn. Unfortunately, funding is short, and the school district only offers reading programs to children up to the third grade," the principal continued. Since so much hinged on Tony's ability to read, Mr. Edwards planned to consult the district office for advice.

For years I had seen but paid little attention to the back-to-school sales. Now all the hype made sense to me. Working mothers can't wash school clothes nightly, so we went on a shopping spree. I'm not sure Tony understood the necessity for more clothing, but making these preparations did increase his excitement about school. He was hesitant about school itself but excited about meeting new friends.

A few days before school started, Tony had been out riding his bike around our now-familiar neighborhood and came in and sat down at the kitchen table. I poured us each a glass of lemonade. "Here, Tony, have a cool drink. You look hot. Where did you ride your bike?"

Never will I understand how Tony's eyes could say so much more than his mouth! "I went to my school." I understood what he said, but I also "heard" his eyes and understood what he didn't say. He was worried about something.

"Oh, so you rode to your school. What did you do over there?"

"Sat on the grass."

"Is that all?" I inquired.

"I just looked at the building. What's for dinner?" He changed the subject, so I let it drop.

Later that night, instead of starting the Bionic Mom routine, he sat quietly and seemed distant. At last his thoughts came to fruition, and he pleaded with me, "Mom, do I have to go to school?"

"Tony, you'll love it, sweets! Just think of all the friends you'll meet! And remember, you're going to learn to read and lots of other things."

"We don't go to school in Mexico," he scoffed, slumping even lower in his chair. "It's not important."

So in simple concepts and words I tried to explain to Tony the value of an education. Going off to a strange school was in his near future and growing up with the ability to earn a living was something he could worry about later, so my logic fell short of its mark. But at least he seemed peaceful enough to enjoy a good night's rest.

The first day of school Tony looked handsome in his new clothes and tennis shoes. I packed him a special lunch and tried in every way to encourage him. However, by the time we walked out the front door, I was as nervous as he was.

"Mom," Tony pleaded again, "do I have to go?" His big brown eyes began to look frantic.

"Yes, son, you have to go. Come on, I'll drive you over and walk you to your class."

Mr. Bradley welcomed Tony and showed him to his desk, in the middle of the classroom.

"Good-bye, Tony. I'll see you this afternoon."

He returned my farewell with one of his looks; I got his message. "How could you do this to me, you traitor? Can't you see I'm scared to death?"

Mr. Bradley walked me to the door, assuring me that Tony would make friends quickly and have a great time. So I left him in the middle of a room full of excited, chattering class-mates and drove to the university.

Hugs and excitement greeted me every step of my way across campus. Tingling with happiness, I drank up the busy socializing. It seemed like years since I'd spoken anything above second-grade English. This was the first time I had been away from Tony in two months.

Faculty and staff greeted me, asking, "How's it going with Tony?" Just as I reached my office, someone called, "Hi, Mom!" It was Dr. Sawtell, a favorite member of the English faculty. He hugged me warmly. No one except Tony and Dr. Grant had called me Mom yet, and it made me feel self-conscious. I had to keep reminding myself that I *was* a mom.

The day was crazy with excitement and good-natured teasing. It was great to be out of the house and back at work.

Time flew; three-thirty was rapidly approaching, and I was eager to see Tony and hear about his day. So directly after class I headed home. This was a first. In the past I had never gone home after work, sometimes not until after the evening bas-ketball game. From the kitchen window I spotted Tony com-ing down the walk trailed by another little boy. They seemed to bounce rather than walk, giggling and wiggling their way through the front door.

"Hi, I'm Donny. I met Tony today at school! He doesn't

speak English, does he? Is he from Mexico? What's he doing here? Is he your son? You live in a neat house. I've never been over here before."

By this time I was giggling too. What a little bundle of energy! Tony's smile spread from ear to ear.

"Hi, Donny. I'm Tony's mom. Hi, Tony. How did your day go?"

"Fine."

"Did you have fun?"

"Well . . ."

Not wanting to acknowledge that he might continue to have any difficulties I said, "It'll get better—and soon."

Donny was still taking in his surroundings. "What a neat place," he said again. Stepping closer, he looked me over carefully and announced, "You don't look like a mom."

"That's okay, Donny, I don't feel like one, either. Maybe that will come later." I winked at Tony. Little did Donny know that this mother-son relationship was new to both of us. "Would you boys like some cookies and milk? Come sit in the kitchen." As I poured the milk, I wondered what a mother should look like. "Are you and Tony in the same class, Donny?"

"Yeah, we're in Mr. Bradley's class together," he munched out the words through a mouthful of cookies. "Tony studied math all day! I don't look like I'm in the fifth grade, do I? I'm a runt. And I take tranquilizer pills 'cause I have too much energy." Donny was so comical. You couldn't help but enjoy his enthusiasm. He was just the friend for Tony: outgoing and cheerful and willing to carry on both sides of a conversation.

That first week of school seemed to go fine; Donny helped a lot. Mr. Bradley agreed when I met with him at the end of the week. He was a tall, athletic-looking man who radiated confidence. "Tony's making friends, and he's working hard on his math."

"Actually, he's been complaining to me that *all* he does is math, every day. Isn't there something else he could do for part of the day?"

"It's the reading problem. What can he do if he can't read? We still don't have a solution. Mr. Edwards is pursuing it with the school district."

Mr. Bradley's response was frustrating, so I reminded myself that there were thirty other children in his class and tried to be patient. "We're going to have problems if Tony gets bored," I cautioned.

"Well, Tony's a whiz at math, and I have him helping the other students."

This was reassuring. So far he'd majored in English and the basic mechanics of any household item that could be taken apart. "It's encouraging that Tony is good at math, but I'm really concerned about this reading thing," I persisted.

"You're right, and we're working on a solution. But for now, just relax. He's doing fine."

On my way out I stopped by the principal's office, and since he didn't have any ideas yet, I went to the district office myself. I was told that the only option for Tony was to put him in a class with handicapped children. There he would at least receive individual instruction. No one thought that was the best solution.

Toward the end of the second week, my secretary buzzed me in my office with a call from Tony's principal. The date for Tony's testing must have been arranged, I thought. (Mr. Bradley had suggested having Tony tested to determine his academic and emotional development.)

"Carolyn, just a little while ago, Tony ran out of Mr. Bradley's class and off the school grounds. We thought that you should check at home and see if he's there."

I couldn't get out of the office fast enough. Why would he leave school? Was he sick? On the way home I swung by the park on the off chance he'd gone there. He hadn't. Frantically I pulled the car into the garage and ran up the walk. Immediately I sensed something wrong. All the drapes were tightly drawn, and the deadbolt on the front door was pulled.

There was an eerie feeling about the darkened house. "Tony, are you here?" I called. I went in.

A look of terror on Tony's face brought me quickly to the sofa, where he was curled into a fetal position, clinging to a pile of pillows.

"Tony, what happened?"

Mingled sweat and tears rolled down his face, and in a fit of uncontrollable trembling, he began to shout, "Make him stop yelling! Make him stop yelling! I can't stand it! It's just like prison!" he sobbed.

All of this came through stuttering and hysteria. "What are you talking about, Tony?" I wrapped him in my arms—giving him a little protection in a world that seemed so terrifying.

"Mom, it's just like prison! Make him stop yelling! I can't stand it!" Over and over he continued his pleading until his eyes flashed wildly around the living room as if in search of an escape.

"Tony, Tony!" I shook him lightly. "Look at me. Tell me what's wrong, Tony!"

"Mr. Bradley," he managed. "He yells at us. He yells at us just like in prison. Mom, Mom, make him stop!"

Tony was too far gone for reason. I just rocked him in my arms until he began to relax. "Son," I spoke gently, "Your school is not a prison, and no one is going to hit you."

I knew that, in Tony's mind, Mr. Bradley had become Senor Manuel at La Granja, where hitting had always followed yelling. The hurt and pain of his past had left him little reserve for dealing with conflict.

I had a feeling that teaching Tony new things was going to be a lot easier than teaching him to effectively deal with the pain of his past. How I wished that he could forget Senor Manuel and the prison!

Chapter Seventeen

The yelling in Mr. Bradley's class had disturbed Tony tremendously. For the rest of the evening he would hardly let me out of his sight. He seemed embarrassed—maybe for letting his emotions be seen—and very withdrawn. As far as Tony was concerned, he never wanted to see his school again. It wasn't any different than the prison in his eyes, and he was bored anyway. Since the next day was Friday and I didn't teach, keeping Tony with me in the office seemed like a good idea. My student staff would enjoy having Tony around, and it wouldn't hurt him to miss class on Friday and let this episode blow over.

After calling Mr. Edwards and making an appointment for Monday morning, I leaned back in my chair feeling very, very tired. The walls of my study were lined with books. How wonderful it would be if I could pull a book off the shelf and discover how to handle this situation. Loneliness seeped into the cracks of my unseasoned mothering, and I reached for the phone.

"Hi Alva," I said, trying to sound happy. "Do you have a minute?"

She did, indeed, and so much wisdom about little boys that her confidence was catching. She simply encouraged me to keep on loving him and building our relationship. "Carolyn, you're going to make it; you're doing just fine."

What beautiful, reassuring words. I hung up the phone and started dinner. Instead of watching television as he usually did at this time, Tony huddled in a corner of the kitchen watching me.

On Saturday morning, Tony was still moping around the house. He let me out of his sight only for a few minutes of bike riding, returning to check on me at short intervals. By now,

we were like Siamese twins; I was beginning to feel smothered. Once again, excesses—just like his showering, eating,
and playing, he now needed excessive mothering.

"Tony, how about going for a bike ride over to your
school or down to the park?"

"No. I don't want to."

"I need to go to the market, why don't you go see Donny
while I shop? Donny keeps asking you to go over to his house
and play."

"No, I don't want to."

Desperately, I searched for a way to get out of the house
for a few hours and do some much-needed shopping. "Then
how about going to the market with me?"

"I don't like the market, too many people. Can't you find
a market without people?"

Sometimes mothering Tony was like driving the car with
the brake set. All my efforts met with resistance.

"Okay, if you don't want to go to the market, we'll have
to go out to dinner tonight."

"No, I don't like restaurants. There are always too many
people. I like it here, and I don't want to go. I don't like to
go out."

Awakening on Monday morning, I felt relief at the
thought of going back to work. But Tony could hardly be
coaxed out of bed. He didn't need to be reminded that we had
an appointment to see Mr. Edwards and Mr. Bradley.

At the meeting both men were very friendly and encouraging and worked hard to ease Tony back into the classroom.
Finally he seemed comfortable enough to go to class with Mr.
Bradley. I sketched out a little of Tony's background for Mr.
Edwards, carefully exchanging "institution" for "prison" and
explaining that he'd been there because he'd been abandoned,
not wanting anyone to overreact to him. I hoped what I'd told
him would help them better understand Tony's behavior.

A friend who was a bilingual teacher in a neighboring
town agreed to evaluate Tony's progress in English. Janice's

crisp Spanish carried from the study to the kitchen where I worked. She and Tony became instant friends, and I could see that she'd have his full cooperation. They worked and played through the testing for an hour and a half and emerged relaxed and smiling.

"I have some news for you, Carolyn." She accepted coffee, and we seated ourselves around the kitchen table. "How long has Tony been with you?"

I figured for a moment. "Three and a half months."

"Tony is speaking better English in three and a half months than most of the students in my class are after three or four years. You can be very proud of him. How did you bring him this far?"

"It's either sink or swim around home," I laughed. "And no one at church or school speaks Spanish, so he can't fall back on Spanish there either."

"That's probably the secret, but he has still progressed beyond what I would expect. He's bright, Carolyn."

Tony came grinning around the corner. He had obviously been listening, and I was pleased that he could feel really good about himself, even for only a short time.

School continued to be a problem, and so did the yelling. Tony and Donny continued to complain about Mr. Bradley. "Mom, you've got to make him stop yelling. That's all he does is yell."

"Come on, it can't be that bad!" Surely he had blown it out of proportion.

But Donny was always ready to play defense attorney. He would take a John Wayne stance with his hands on his hips: "They do yell, Carolyn. They yell all the time. It's just terrible!"

Getting Tony off to school grew more and more difficult. "School is boring, Mom. All I do is math. They won't teach me anything. Don't they do anything but math in the United States?"

Mr. Bradley had seemed interested in Tony, so I decided

to go see him again. About twenty minutes before school was out, I approached the open door of his classroom. The boisterous students could be heard all the way down the corridor, but Mr. Bradley's yelling outvoiced them all. Donny and Tony had been right. This huge hulk of a man brought a ruler crashing down upon a desktop in hopes of gaining control, but the silence lasted only as long as the students' short-lived shock.

There was Tony in the back of the room, sweat pouring down his face, grasping his desk, both hands white-knuckled. As an educator, I knew how detrimental tension was to learning, and I also knew the joy of a happy classroom. But as a mother, I saw it all through Tony's eyes and knew that he expected this new "Senor Manuel" to club him or backhand him at any moment.

As the bell rang, a stampede of excited children nearly trampled me. "Mr. Bradley," I began. "Tony is bored; he's also a nervous wreck due to all the yelling in this classroom."

"The students are always excitable. He'll just have to get used to it. This is just part of Tony's very important socialization process. Did he spend a lot of time alone in the institution?"

How could I answer that question? "Mr. Bradley, Tony is bored with school and I can hardly force him to come. What can we do to stimulate his interest?"

"As I've told you, this city isn't funded to deal with Tony's kind of reading problem. I don't know what we can do except continue with his studies in math and encourage his socialization."

I sensed his concern as he tried to somehow console me. "Mr. Bradley, I realize Tony has some unique problems—" Just at that moment, Mr. Edwards walked in.

"Hello, Carolyn, I am so glad you've come by. The school district has arranged for a battery of comprehensive tests to be done on Tony next week. How does that sound?" he smiled.

"Just great! At least we'll know for sure what his capabilities are and where to begin."

"He will be tested by three psychologists, one of whom is bilingual so that the test can be given orally. His English is coming along fine, but he couldn't be fairly evaluated in English yet. They also warned me," Mr. Edwards cautioned, "that the test is geared toward North American culture so not to expect too much from him."

The day of the test was a little frightening for me. What if he flunked? What if . . . ? When he came in after school that day obviously relaxed, my own tension eased. "How did the testing go, Tony?"

"Oh, not too bad," he shrugged his shoulders. "They asked me lots of questions. Can I have something to eat?"

"Sure, I'm a little hungry too. What did you think of their questions?" I pried.

Tony wiped his milky mustache on his arm. "I just answered them, Mom."

The following Wednesday I waited outside the principal's office while he conferred with the three psychologists. When he noticed I had arrived he immediately invited me to join them. "The test scores are ready, and we're trying to decide what to do about them."

"What do you mean?" I asked.

"We would like to inform you, Miss Koons," one of the psychologists began, "that your son's test scores placed him at the top of the scale; he qualifies for the mentally gifted program in our district!"

"He *what!*" I gasped, and they all laughed.

"That's right, Carolyn," said Mr. Edwards bubbling with enthusiasm. "His test scores are that of a seventeen year old, a senior in high school."

"Here is our recommendation, Miss Koons," the psychologist said eagerly. "We would like to put him into our program for gifted children. These kids have a unique educational experience; they visit museums and the zoo, then they write reports and—"

"But Tony can hardly write his own name," I broke in.

"He can't read at all; he'd be lost with the gifted children. Let's just teach him the basics for now—like reading and writing!"

The psychologist couldn't believe that I didn't want more for my son. "Tony doesn't qualify for the reading program; he should be with the mentally gifted children."

Tony never seemed to fit the patterns. I was beginning to feel as though I was back in Mexicali at the birth certificate office. "I'm proud of Tony and grateful to you for your generous offer, but I just don't think it fits his needs."

Mr. Edwards joined in. "I'll have to agree with Carolyn; there's got to be something more appropriate for Tony. Let's go back to the district again and see what can be done."

Tony was developing a deep resentment of school. Passing his classroom on the way to my car I heard Mr. Bradley's voice again, raised enough to be heard above the rowdy students. Judging by Tony's expression, a storm was brewing, and it couldn't be far off!

Tony wasn't the only one with problems. It was very difficult for me to keep my mind on my work at the university. Part of the trouble was that two and three times a week I had to meet with someone at Tony's school or at the district office. Always I had to be home with him by three-thirty. I crammed all my work into a shortened day and hurried home to my little recluse of a son. I noticed that he was beginning to become more moody.

One day late in October, I walked into my office just in time to answer the phone.

"Hello Carolyn, this is Mr. Edwards. There's been a problem here at school with Tony, and we need to talk to you immediately."

"What happened?" I asked.

"Please, come over to the school and we'll talk."

My secretary canceled two meetings and I left immediately. Donny was waiting for me in the school's parking lot.

"I told him not to do it!" Donny was jumping up and down, almost screaming and so hysterical that I could hardly understand him. "I told Tony not to hit Mr. Bradley," he cried.

"Donny, calm down. Everything's going to be just fine. Go back to the classroom and we'll talk later. Scoot now." I turned him gently toward his room.

Tony's scowl met me as I walked into the office. Kneeling down beside his chair, I whispered, "Hello, son, can you tell me what happened?" He didn't try to answer.

Clearing his throat, Mr. Edwards entered the room and motioned toward his office. "I would like to see you both in here." Mr. Bradley was close on our heels and closed the door soundly behind us.

A sick feeling of dread did nasty things to my already upset stomach. "Carolyn, Tony will have to be suspended for two days."

"What happened?" I asked.

"He was chewing gum. Mr. Bradley told him that it was against our rules and that he should throw it away. With that, Tony defiantly put his hands on his hips and said, 'You make me!' "

"Is that right, Tony?" I questioned.

He looked down and nodded.

"Then, when I put my hand on his shoulder," Bradley's voice sounded a little hoarse, "he hit me as hard as he could and took off running. I was able to grab him and bring him here."

Where on earth did Tony get the nerve to hit giant Mr. Bradley? What kind of little monster did I have on my hands?

Just as we reached our front porch, I heard Donny's high-pitched voice following us down the walk.

"What happened? Did you get kicked out of school? It wasn't his fault, Carolyn; it was a set-up! It really was!" he blurted out.

"Donny, slow down! What do you mean, 'set-up'?"

"A couple of guys gave Tony a whole pack of gum at recess

and told him that they wanted him to be their friend. Then they asked him if he could chew the whole pack." Donny's eyes were enormous with expression. "I *told* him not to do it." Angrily his little fists came down at his sides and he stomped his foot. "Why wouldn't he listen?"

"Then what happened?"

"They told him that mean old Mr. Bradley would take it away from him because he didn't want Tony to have new friends. When Bradley tried to get him to spit out the gum, Tony really freaked out! He hit Bradley really hard and even tried to karate-kick him!"

I groaned. "What a mess!"

Punishment seemed irrelevant, somehow. The problem was far too complicated. Emotionally damaged, Tony was conditioned to survive at any cost. Prayer was the only hope. "God, just as you helped me, please help my son to let go of his terrifying past."

Chapter Eighteen

Tony had two worlds, one was mostly happy and the other was mostly not. He loved being home playing in the house and tinkering in the garage. He still enjoyed taking things apart, but now, at least, he could put most of them back together. We really enjoyed each other's company and had a lot of fun doing little projects around the house. Both Tony and I were becoming a little more comfortable in our roles of mother and son.

Tony also loved soccer. It made his other world, school, almost tolerable. Back during the second or third week of school, Donny and Tony had come home especially happy.

"Guess what, Mom?" Tony practically sang. "They're starting soccer teams, and lots of kids in my class are signing up." He handed me an application and almost sat on my lap to make sure that he had my full attention. "Can I play? Soccer's a Mexican game. All Mexicans know how to play soccer. I'm really good."

Quickly I read the information. "Tony, this sounds terrific. I'd love for you to play." Both Donny and Tony jumped up and down enthusiastically. "You realize they require two soccer practices and a game every Saturday?" Tony was ecstatic and watched me as I filled out every line of the application.

"A real Mexican soccer player! Hey, Tony!" Donny chattered and danced all around the kitchen. "I'll be at all your games and all your practices too. You're going to win 'cause you're a real Mexican soccer player!"

Tony's chest puffed up with pride; he could hardly wait to make Donny's predictions come true.

When Tuesday rolled around, my half-pint soccer player and his would-be trainer went off to practice. Tony couldn't wait to play, and Donny couldn't wait to watch. The coach gave each of the boys a beautiful royal blue shirt with matching socks and white shorts. Tony was number five. Getting his very own soccer uniform almost overwhelmed him. We went shopping for soccer shoes that very day and talked about soccer that night at bedtime instead of Mr. Bradley and math.

After the second week of practice, Tony came home very frustrated. "That coach keeps making up rules, all kinds of rules, for our soccer game. Soccer doesn't have lots of rules. You just play the game."

"Of course there are rules, Tony."

"No, there aren't! I've played for years, and I know the rules." He pounded his chest. "There aren't very many of them. He keeps telling us that we have to play a certain way; 'you can do this stuff and you can't do some other stuff.' I know the rules. It's a Mexican game and I'm a Mexican!"

I grinned and thought of the games we had watched in Mexico. There was a lot of pushing but even more laughing. "Tony, you're right. Americans do play soccer differently, but I think that the professional teams in Mexico play exactly the way the Americans play." The discipline of learning to play within the rules and playing with team feeling would be good for Tony.

Although he didn't like the rules, Tony did learn to play by them. Soccer was a Mexican game, and he would pay the cost, whatever it was, for the chance to play his national sport.

The morning of Tony's first game, he got up early and dressed himself in his uniform hours before the game. He wanted to be ready on time. When we arrived, colorfully dressed teams were working on pregame warm-ups as proud parents mingled on the sidelines. Laughing inwardly at my shyness, I awkwardly joined the group and found them very friendly. Several women identified themselves and pointed out their children, so I pointed out mine.

"Oh, so you're Tony's mother."

"We think it's great that there's a boy from Mexico on the team!"

Tony seemed to lack concentration on the game. If the ball came to him he kicked it enthusiastically; otherwise he seemed to be daydreaming. It was hard not to yell, "Hey, Koons, wake up!" I wished Tony would catch some team spirit, but he was content to just enjoy the game. No one criticized him. I realized that during Tony's prison days, it had been strictly every boy for himself. If you survived, even a soccer game, it was because you looked out for yourself.

By the end of the season he was talking about joining Little League baseball and maybe even basketball later in the year.

Sports made a tremendous difference in Tony's outlook on life and helped him make it through some unbearable days of school. Soccer indirectly helped me as well. All the frustration that he worked out on the field might otherwise have been taken out on me. So in spite of all the "dumb" rules, Tony had a good soccer season, with Mom and Donny cheering him on from the sidelines.

On Saturdays, we came home from the game, he changed and ate, then he became quietly involved with little projects in the house or garage. I had feared the struggle we would have if he had turned out to be messy, but, thank God, it never materialized. From the very beginning he was neat and or-derly. On the second morning he was home I went into his room and gave him careful instructions for making his own bed; he watched attentively. After that, whenever I passed his room in the morning, his bed was neatly made. Occasionally he needed reminders about tools in the garage, but that was all.

As orderly as he kept his room, I did notice a progressive accumulation of junk, an immaculately organized hoard of worthless junk. If I dared to suggest that he throw something away, he responded as if I were trying to take his most prized possession. Papers, rubber bands, empty boxes—anything that was once useful was considered worth saving for the future. He was quickly becoming a packrat, par excellence.

In the past, I had read or heard about people that saved everything, and had never understood why someone would do that. With Tony, though, I realized it was a carry-over from prison days and talked myself into trying to ignore it until the major issues in our lives were more settled. If it went on too much longer, however, we would have to get another house just for his junk!

Week in and out, school remained the dreaded obstacle to Tony's happiness. The school was still trying to figure out how to handle this mentally gifted student who couldn't read or write but managed to excel in math. I tried to work with Tony at home as much as possible, but spending most of his day in school, then coming home to more work did not sit well with him. His vociferous complaints wore me down terribly. I had never liked conflict, and having it in my own home was deadly. I must have dreaded Tony's homework sessions as much as he did. His iron will was doing more than trying my patience; it was beginning to tear away part of me.

Tony continued to help the weaker students in math, while several strong readers started using flash-card drills with him. Between school and home we nearly flash-carded him to death. Each day he worked on twenty-five new words.

Dr. Grant's wife, Pauline, was a kindergarten teacher, and she began working with Tony several times a week. Her special reading method and spelling program created a fun game that taught Tony valuable skills. Best of all, it was great to have a friend step in and help so that mother didn't have to be teacher-tutor too.

Because Tony was smart it was easy to expect too much. I needed to continually remind myself to be patient. For Tony's intelligence and all the fun times we shared together, I thanked God. The roughest part of our journey seemed to be behind us.

Chapter Nineteen

Activities mushroomed in every corner of my office as plans jelled for Mexicali Outreach this Easter week. We were expecting to take one thousand young people from Azusa Pacific University and various West Coast churches. I loved the challenge of directing this program. No one had benefited more from it than I had.

The last person I wanted to hear from that early December morning was Tony's principal, but as I answered the phone, I instantly recognized his voice.

"Carolyn, Tony came to school this morning but then took off on his bike. Will you please go home and see if he's there?"

It was only nine o'clock. He couldn't have stayed at school more than thirty minutes. "What happened? Did he and Mr. Bradley get into it again?"

"No, Carolyn. This time he hit me!"

"Oh no," I moaned, "you've got to be kidding! What happened?"

"Why don't you go find him first. Then the two of you can come back to school and we'll talk."

Once again I turned to my secretary, "Sonja, cancel my meetings. I have to go find Tony, *again.* He just clobbered the principal and took off on his bike." She winced sympathetically.

On the way home I passed the park and scanned it for my wayward son. This time my detour paid off. Tony was sitting on his bike watching some older boys shoot baskets. He heard my call from across the field and rode his bike toward the car as if nothing at all had happened. But as he came closer and saw the serious look on my face, he drew back a bit.

"Why aren't you in school?" I demanded.

"It's just a bunch of rules," he objected. "That's all this

country is—just a bunch of rules." I was getting awfully tired of hearing him say that whenever he ran head-on into the system, but I knew I needed to hear him out before jumping to conclusions.

"Why? What happened?"

"Mom, I didn't know, and they said I couldn't ride my bike to school!" he responded frantically.

"Wait one minute! Why can't you ride your bike to school?"

"I don't know." He stuttered and stammered, nearly unintelligible. "They said I can't ride my bike."

"Tony, ride your bike home, we're going to see Mr. Edwards."

"Do I have to go?"

"Yes son, we have to go."

The crossing guard, in full uniform, awaited our arrival in the principal's office.

"We seem to have a problem here, Carolyn," Mr. Edwards began.

I remained quiet and tried to listen.

"We have a traffic problem in front of the school, so this week we hired a crossing guard. One of his jobs is to enforce the rule against riding bikes in the crosswalk."

"Yes," the crossing guard contributed, "and Tony didn't get off, he rode his bike."

"So what happened then?" I asked.

"I told him to get off and walk it, and when he didn't, I yelled at him to get off his bike. But he just rode all the faster."

"This is where I come in," the principal said. "When I saw him fly into the bike racks and tear off toward his classroom, I called after him—not knowing what had happened, of course. He did stop for a moment, then started running again. When I finally caught up with him and grabbed his shoulder, he instantly turned and slugged me with all his strength." Mr. Edwards's indignation was mounting. "We cannot have Tony hitting people, Carolyn!"

"Tony was wrong, Mr. Edwards," I said wearily. "I'll talk with him some more."

At this point, I seriously considered telling him and the whole school about La Granja—how Tony had had to hit and run as fast as he could to protect himself from the older boys and Senor Manuel. He'd understand if he heard about all the awful beatings. But on reflection, I knew it wouldn't help. Tony's past didn't justify the present; it only helped explain it. I kept my mouth shut.

As we drove home Tony began his explanation. "Mom, I didn't *know* I had to walk my bike across the street. Nobody ever told me. I don't have to walk my bike at the corner by our house, so why should I have to walk it just one block down the street?"

He seemed sincerely confused. "All people do here is make up rules! In Mexico we don't have rules. We don't have to walk our bikes in Mexico; why do we have to here?" Tony became more agitated with every word. "It's just rules, dumb rules!"

"Tony, settle down and listen! Walking your bike across the street is a simple rule and will not inconvenience you very much. The school is only trying to control the traffic so that no one gets hurt. But the *real* problem is that you ran from the crossing guard and the principal and then hit the principal. Why did you feel you had to hit him, Tony?"

He hung his head, "I don't know why I hit him."

I spoke to him softly but firmly, "Tony, you've spent years in prison fighting and hitting, but that's behind you. Leave it, Tony, and move on with your life. Don't let your past mess up your chance to be happy today!" It was a simple statement. But if it could be learned it would be the key to turning Tony's life around.

At home I imposed as few rules as possible but made sure that each one was carried out consistently. Together we made progress, but the tension grew between Tony and his teacher. What was the problem? Was it Mr. Bradley's yelling in class, or were we dealing with a struggle against authority figures? Perhaps school just seemed boring? Or was it a problem of culture shock, of learning a whole new system of rules? I couldn't seem to get a handle on it, and it threatened to overwhelm me.

One afternoon, Tony was forty-five minutes late coming home from school. Since as a rule I could set my watch by him, my anxiety mounted. I was standing at the kitchen window when he finally came, Donny trailing along behind. Instead of coming into the kitchen and talking about their day, they quickly whizzed by me and headed up the stairs. Something was wrong.

"What's up, guys?" I called after them.

"Nothing!" Tony yelled, slamming his bedroom door.

Well, they would spill their story in due time, I thought, and went on fixing dinner. I wasn't totally surprised when the principal called. "Would you please come right over to my office—without Tony." It was more an order than a request.

I knocked on Tony's door and then went in. "Mr. Edwards just called; he wants to see me." Their two little faces looked uneasy. "I'll be back in a short while. Stay put, okay? I don't want you to go outside until I get back."

A distraught woman was sitting in Mr. Edwards's office when I arrived.

"Carolyn, this is Mrs. DeArmond. Her son attends our school."

I nodded but didn't speak; Mr. Edwards seemed more like an angry panther than himself.

"You're both acquainted with Donny Miller, I believe? He's the focal point of this incident." Mr. Edwards shuddered and crossed his arms over his chest in what seemed like an effort to control his rage.

"Apparently, on the way home from school three boys—one of whom was your son, Mrs. DeArmond—jumped Donny, and began to hit him and knock him around."

"You realize how small Donny is, don't you, Mrs. DeArmond?" Mr. Edwards released his breath like a hot pressure cooker and jerked his body to face my direction. Here goes, I thought.

"Miss Koons, this is where your son comes into the picture. He was following a little behind Donny, and when the other boys jumped on him, Tony ran to his defense. Within minutes he had sent all three boys sprawling—especially Mrs. DeArmond's son, who, by the way, had to be taken to the emergency room. He has a mild concussion and a tennis shoe mark on the side of his head!" His eyes and words pierced my body. "Are you aware that Tony uses karate, Carolyn?"

"No, I didn't have any idea." I was both shocked and embarrassed. "I'm very sorry your son was injured, Mrs. DeArmond." She didn't respond, but the look on her face was one of disdain and outrage. I had the feeling she would have liked to ask why I'd brought this violent, lower-class animal into our peaceful upper-middle-class Glendora community.

"Tony will be suspended from school for the rest of this week and all of next week, and I don't want him anywhere near the school." By this time Mr. Edwards had stood and sat by turns several times, trying to relieve the pressure of his emotions. The room seemed smaller all the time. "Tony is becoming more violent, and I want him off the streets. If you don't keep him off the streets," the principal warned, "I will notify the juvenile authorities!"

Mrs. DeArmond finally broke her icy silence. "I've heard about your son," she retorted. "If anything else happens to my son, I will report Tony to the police myself. He belongs in juvenile hall!"

I walked to my car in a trance. Karate! Karate seemed so violent! What else did he know? The thought of having Tony reported to the juvenile authorities terrified me. How could I teach my classes and keep Tony off the streets and the juvenile authorities off our doorstep? Feeling painfully lonely and overwhelmed, I just sat there. Every inch of my body ached. Oh God, I needed a break! I needed someone to just hold me and tell me that everything was going to be okay.

But there was no one there; I was on my own. I managed

to start the car and headed home to face Tony.

The boys were nervously waiting for me on the couch. Outwardly calm, but still angry and depressed, I asked them to explain what had happened.

"Those idiots would have knocked my brains out, but Tony saved me." Donny's hero worship made Tony sit up a little straighter.

I explained what Tony's kick had done to the DeArmond boy and that a concussion was a serious injury. "The principal has decided to suspend you from school for a week and a half, Tony."

"But, Mom," he pleaded, "why?"

Donny's voice became shrill, "Yeah, why Tony? Why don't they suspend the boys who started the fight?"

"Boys, I know they were wrong to start the fight, but, Tony, you are suspended for using a karate kick." I was beginning to feel a little confused myself. "If you had started this fight, Tony, I would have been very upset, but as it stands, I'm proud of you for defending your friend. What concerns me, though, is that you know how to use karate. Do you realize how dangerous that is, Tony?"

He merely shrugged. It was hard for Tony to understand. He felt condemned for doing what was right, while the truly guilty ones got off scot-free. It wouldn't make things at school any easier for him. Although it was becoming increasingly difficult for me to juggle my two worlds, I cut my work back even more and spent as much time with Tony as possible. I constantly worked with him on controlling his fighting—especially his use of karate, but Tony often expressed frustration with the "worthless rules" he had to learn; people here didn't understand things the way the people in Mexico did.

When he got really worked up, his stuttering became worse; sometimes he could hardly speak. I had had the same problem in junior high. Now, the more Tony stuttered, the more I stuttered. Sometimes I was able to laugh at myself, but it didn't help. For the most part it was quite embarrassing, especially during lectures.

Worse than my feeling of helplessness was the loneliness. More than anything, I wanted to talk over our problems with one of my friends. "You'll never make it, Carolyn": those words haunted me. I wouldn't share my problems with anyone. My friends might begin to think that she was right. I had to make it. I couldn't fail!

Where were all those people who had said they would take Tony fishing, or to a Dodger's game, or anywhere? Everybody seemed very busy in their own little worlds, unaware of my muffled plea for help. Some days I found myself praying to be away from him for a little while to regain my composure and retrieve my self-respect. But this particular phase of our journey was a very lonely one.

Our best time was after Tony crawled into bed each night. I would come in and sit with him for a long talk. I encouraged him to talk through his feelings and frustrations, and he tried.

"I don't know why I get mad and fight. Why do I do these dumb things?" he questioned with intense frustration. "If God really loved me, he wouldn't let me do these things! If God is so strong, why doesn't he stop me?" With a pleading look, he would try to draw strength from me to meet his overwhelming problems. "Mom, I don't know how to be good. I don't want to be in trouble all the time!"

"Tony, you're doing great. I'm very proud of you. You've had a lot of things to *un*learn along with all the new things to learn. You're doing fine!" We prayed together and asked God to help us. Tony stuttered through his prayer, begging God to make him a good boy.

Finally, he would receive my words of encouragement and relax, thinking that tomorrow would be a better day.

Chapter Twenty

Just days before the Christmas recess, Mr. Edwards and I agreed that Tony needed a fresh start, a new school. I had been wondering if a private Christian school might be a better environment for him, anyway. Tony certainly didn't complain when I told him that he wouldn't be going back to Mr. Bradley's class.

Christmas vacation came as rain on parched ground for the Koons family. After the chaos and pressure of the preceding month, we looked forward to spending the holiday with Grandma and Grandpa Peters up in the mountains.

Christmas carolers chorused up and down the mall where we went to do some shopping before our trip. Tony could hardly take it all in. We shopped, then ate, then shopped some more, dragging our growing mound of packages from store to store. In front of one store was a beautiful, snowy Christmas scene, in reality, electrically animated characters playing in finely grated Styrofoam. Tony hung on the banister enclosing the scene and studied every detail, then dropped his hand down to finger the snow. He meticulously examined it, letting it run through his fingers several times. After a long pause for thought, he reached his hand out to show me. "So this is snow?"

I laughed. "No Tony, it isn't real snow; this only looks like snow!"

A look of confusion crossed his face. "Well, if this isn't snow, what is snow?"

The very next day we joined Barbara and John Fraley and their daughter, Jennifer, and went in search of the real thing. With snow powdered on his cheeks and lashes, teeth chattering, Tony said, "So *this* is snow!" He spent the day throwing snow balls and jumping and sliding into the snow without regard for cold or wet. He abandoned all restraint that day and became freer than I had ever seen him.

The next day we headed up to Grandma and Grandpa's. The Christmas program at Russell's church depicted the birth of Christ our Savior so well that God seemed very near indeed. All the familiar Christmas songs and the pastor's message of hope made me feel as if God really cared about my aching, troubled heart. It was therapeutic to lose myself in the Christmas festivities and the freshness of mountain splendor. Both of us enjoyed that holiday tremendously. The problems of city and school seemed far away.

Russ and Alva's home glowed with Christmas spirit, from the sparkling Christmas tree to the decorations on Grandma's cookies. Tony seemed to inhale love and exhale happiness.

My gift to him that Christmas was a jet black dirt bike, something I knew he'd been wanting, and he rewarded me with that special smile that had been so rare lately. Tony also received a model car, but I doubted he would be able to assemble it, because he couldn't read the detailed instructions. I should have known better: Tony carefully studied the pictures, and within hours, the model was taking shape; by the day after Christmas, each of the hundreds of pieces had been correctly placed and it stood complete.

"Look, Mom, I don't have to go to school and I don't have to read. I put this whole thing together without reading the instructions," he boasted.

Renewed in body and spirit, we returned home ready to begin again. I decided on Tony's new school and called to enroll him as a sixth-grader. Everything was up front this time: I had been a guest speaker at the church that sponsored the school about a year before Tony came home. At that time all we knew was that he had been sold into slave labor. I had told them about his troubled history and asked for their prayers.

Tony came home that first day with a new optimism. He reported that the new school had a healthy mix of blacks, Mexicans, and whites; he no longer felt conspicuous for his race. And—praise God—he seemed to have taken a shine to Mrs. Spurling, who taught his special reading class of only fifteen students. After thirty-five years on the mission field, she was giving her life to the children, and there was something about her that made them want to do their best.

Her classroom was slightly separated from the other classes and had a relaxed, homey atmosphere. With her gray hair in a neat bun on the nape of her neck, fresh and bright in one of her two dresses, she greeted each child with a cheery hug. Tony couldn't stop talking about her.

"Mom, I have a new teacher, like a grandma. I like her. She's kind of like the old lady I took care of when they sold me from prison."

Although Lupe had found out a little about what had happened during that time, I had never brought the subject up with Tony myself. It was interesting now to hear him speak of it.

"Where were you all that time, Tony?"

"Oh, I was in Santa Barbara," he recalled easily. "They snuck me across the border under a blanket in the backseat of a car. Everyone pretended like they were asleep."

"So what did you do in Santa Barbara?"

"I worked in the fields a little, but most of the time I took care of an old lady because she was very sick. That was my job."

"Did you like her, Tony?"

"She was my friend . . ." His voice trailed off and he looked sad.

Lupe had discovered that the old woman had died while in Tony's care. It would have been good for him to talk about it, but I decided to wait until Tony brought it up himself.

"Would you like to show me your books?" He still looked pensive and sad. "Tony, did Mrs. Spurling give you a book?"

This time he responded and pushed a book toward me, "She gave me two books. I'm going to read this one, and the other one is a spelling book."

"Are you sure that she didn't give you four math books?" I teased.

"No way! And guess what—I even know some of my spelling words."

Proudly Tony took the book and demonstrated his new skills. It was hard to believe that he was excited about anything related to school.

Just as we were talking, Mrs. Spurling called and told me how much she had enjoyed having Tony in her class that day. She explained that he had a reading clinic for an hour a day with another teacher and that he should read half an hour each night.

Tony liked to read for a half an hour about as much as a cat likes a bath. How he fought me! I wished for a shot we could inject him with and program him for reading. But there wasn't one, so we fought on and read every single night.

The sense of kinship between Tony and Mrs. Spurling grew steadily. She sensed Tony's lawless spirit and loved it; to her it was a source of great potential. She was wise to his ways and handled him so smoothly that he never realized he'd been handled. She sensed his feelings and could help him move through his frustrations.

The roots of many of Tony's conflicts gradually began to be exposed. One major problem he had was his lack of respect for male authority, especially angry authority. He responded very well to the men who were friendly and even-tempered. This resentment seemed to stem from the brutality of the guards at La Granja and, even before, that of his own step-father. If anyone lost their temper, Tony became indignant, yet his own fuse was very short. Occasionally, I pointed this out to him, and he acted really surprised at his own behavior. But he gradually began to learn to see his own faults.

One day Tony came home from school angry; it seemed like good therapy for him to vent his feelings, and also it gave me an opportunity to direct his interpretations, so I encouraged him to talk.

"You know, Mom, one time when my dad was really mad at me," he recalled, "he chained my arm to the bed and started hitting me with another chain that had a lock on the end." He pulled up his shirt and exposed his scarred back. "That's where he hit me, and on my legs too. He hated me bad." Tony's face contorted; the pain of his memories was still very real.

"Did he hurt your hand too?" I asked, touching his badly scarred fingers.

"No, that was my mom. If I didn't do something, she got real mad, and one day she put my hand in the fire."

"Tony, you mean to tell me that she burned your hand?"

"Yes, you should have seen it. My fingers were all kind of burned together and my hand was as big as a baseball."

No wonder Tony had no respect for authority. He often said, "All adults do is push you around." Now I saw that in his case that was true. How naive I had been to think that he would automatically love and trust me!

The more I came to know about Tony's past the more significant each step of his progress became. Actually, it was surprising that he could function in the American society at all. But, maybe God knew that Tony could have never made behavioral changes within his own culture and that a completely new environment was to his advantage.

Mrs. Spurling called frequently with good reports about Tony's progress, especially in spelling. Nearly every week he scored 100 percent on his test. The words seemed to come fairly easy to him. In fact, I was surprised at how fast he spelled them back to me when we practiced. One morning at breakfast I noticed one of Tony's spelling words on the cereal box. I pointed it out. "Tony, read this word for me."

He looked blank. "I don't know that word. I've never seen it before."

"Sure you have, Tony. It was on your spelling list about two weeks ago."

"Oh, well, I don't *learn* those words, Mom. I just learn how to spell them."

I grinned in question. "What do you mean, 'you just learn to spell them'? How can you do that?"

"It's real easy, Mom. I'll show you." He handed me his spelling book and said, "Turn to any chapter. Read me the first word." Carefully, I pronounced the word *avenue*.

Tony proceeded to write that word and each of the following twenty-four words, almost perfectly, without my ever reading beyond the first word. When he finished, I pointed to word number twenty. "What is this word, Tony?"

"I don't know! I can't read that word, Mom. I just know how to spell it."

"What do you mean you can't read it? How did you know how to spell it?"

"That's easy. I just memorized all the letters."

"I looked at him to see if he was kidding. Pointing to the letter *J*, I asked, "What's this letter?"

"Uh-uh-uh," he stuttered, "I don't know."

"Tony, do you mean that you memorize all the words letter by letter without knowing the words *or* the letters?"

"Yep, it works!"

"But Tony, what if Mrs. Spurling mixed the words up?"

"I can't do it that way, Mom, 'cause I don't know the words."

For Tony to figure out such an elaborate system for learning so little took a bit of genius. Thereafter, when we studied spelling I mixed up the words and messed up the system. Boy, was I a traitor!

After the first few weeks at the new school Tony became progressively quieter. But he did enjoy talking about Mrs. Spurling. "Mom, why don't we have Mrs. Spurling over for dinner?" He was serious. "Why don't we buy her a new dress? You know, she only has two dresses." It was refreshing to see the tender side of my little fighter. But it didn't last long; soon he fell into his old pattern of complaining about school. Going to work at the university was a welcome relief from Tony's whining.

The second semester at the university was well under way. The first semester had become a blur; I could hardly remember teaching at all. Chatting with my secretary, I commented, "It's such a relief, Sonja, to have Tony in this new school. He still doesn't like school, but at least the principal isn't calling me down there a couple of times a week."

Almost immediately, the telephone rang. "Mexicali Outreach, this is Sonja." She paused. "Just one moment, please." She looked at me apologetically. "Carolyn, it's Mr. Cook, the principal at Tony's school. He wants to know if you can go over to the school and talk with him."

My heart sank. "Yes, set up an appointment for right after class." The brief honeymoon was over. What could be the problem now? Tony was more moody than he had been after Christmas, but he still seemed to be doing much better.

The class I taught was a total blur. I don't even remember what we discussed. My mind was on Tony.

"We are terribly sorry to call you here like this, Carolyn," Mr. Cook began, "but Tony has been talking back to his teachers and ditching reading clinic regularly. He does listen to Mrs. Spurling, though," he added positively. "But this morning, Tony deliberately disrupted Mr. Lacy's class by bouncing a ball against the wall." Tony attended Mr. Lacy's regular sixth-grade class for about an hour each day. "When Mr. Lacy asked Tony to put the ball away and quit disturbing the class, he put his hands on his hips and defiantly yelled back, 'You make me!' "

I cringed at the sound of those familiar words.

"He also got into a fight today, Carolyn. He's had several fights within the last few weeks."

"When did this start? I didn't even know there was a problem!"

"His rebellion has been kind of progressive. We've really tried to deal with it without involving you—we know how much stress you've been under—but Tony is beginning to get out of hand. We need to work together on bringing him back."

"Thank you for trying to protect me, Mr. Cook." I was barely able to control my tears. "I'm grateful for your concern about Tony and I'm very sorry for the trouble he's causing you. What do you suggest?"

Lately, I had aquired two close friends that never seemed to leave my side. One was Exhaustion and the other, Humility. Exhaustion kept making me run and Humility kept tripping me. I could hardly stand any more.

Mr. Cook called in Mrs. Spurling, Mr. Lacy, and Miss Enterline, Tony's reading clinic teacher, so that we could all plan our strategy together. This created a team feeling that saved me from collapse. Somehow we had to turn Tony's behavior around.

"One more item before you go, Carolyn," Mr. Cook stood and walked me toward the door. "Tony got in a fight this morning and beat a kid up. I was reluctant to tell you this and at first wasn't even going to. But I think that in light of today's conversation with everyone it is best to get everything out into the open. I think Tony needs a break, and I think it would be best if he stayed home the rest of the week."

It was a rough week. I was beginning to resent the fact that Tony interfered with my work at the university. And I was becoming more and more angry with him for acting so insubordinate and cocky. It was a while before I even wanted to talk to him. Gradually, I brought up one problem at a time and we dealt with it and then moved on to the next.

Every day I prayed for my son. He would be so much happier if he liked school and got along with people. "Lord, you know how discouraged I am! Whatever I expected during this first year of adjustment never included anything like this! I'm going to stick it out, Lord, but how much longer will he be so rebellious?" My heart ached.

Tony really struggled to come to grips with his own behavior. He seemed to want to obey and even prayed about it. But when the temptation came to defy authority or to prove how tough he was, he simply couldn't resist.

Because he had been suspended from school, I felt that some kind of restriction at home was not only appropriate but necessary, so I informed him that his bedtime would be nine o'clock, rather than ten—minimal, I thought. He seemed to agree.

Our discussion concluded, we went off to my office. I made sure that he did the work he was missing in class. All that day he acted fine, relieved to be out of school. I, however, felt manipulated; this was exactly what Tony wanted. Tony's suspensions were always harder on me than they were on him.

By 8:30 that evening Tony was cuddled up beside me watching television as I graded papers. During the last, sleepy hour before bedtime, he drank up my affection like a little teddy bear and usually acted younger than his age. Just a few minutes before nine, he got up and walked out of the study. When he came back a few minutes later, I had to look twice to make sure it was the same boy, his face was so stern and hard. Then he walked over to my chair arrogantly and said, "I don't really have to go to bed at nine, do I?"

"Yes, Tony, you do have to go to bed at nine, every night for seven nights."

For a moment he eyed me scornfully, as though I were a cheap replica of nothing, then said, "Oh no, I don't, and you can't make me!"

Trying to keep the lid on things, I ignored his attitude and dealt with his remark. "Yeah, babe, I'm sorry, but your bedtime is nine o'clock, and I won't change my mind."

He stepped forward with clenched fists and blazing eyes. For a moment I thought he was going to hit me. "You can't make me do anything. I don't have to obey you," he spat. "You are not my mom!"

Stay calm, stay calm, I told myself. A lot of things went through my mind, but I knew Tony was just trying to get the upper hand. "No, Tony, I'm not the mom you had as a baby, but because I adopted you—you agreed to the adoption, remember?—I *am* your mom now. And I don't want you to forget it!"

"You still can't make me do anything!"

Astonished by Tony's sudden rage, I just stared firmly at him for a moment. The silence was too much for him; he exploded into a ball of fury.

"I don't have to obey you," he screamed. "I don't have to obey anybody!" Every muscle in his body stood at attention, and the veins on his neck and at his temples pulsed wildly. "And I'm not ever going back to school again. If I have to go, I won't learn. You can't make me. No one can make me do anything." He ran out of the room and around the corner to the staircase, where he threw himself down and continued yelling back at me. "You can't make me! You *can't* make me! I'll *never* obey you. I'll never obey anyone!"

I decided to take Tony by the arm, walk him up to his room, and close the door. Wrong! He had wrapped himself so tightly around the banister that I couldn't budge him at all. I was suddenly furious. We were both at the breaking point.

"Tony, why do you keep fighting everyone? We want to help you, not hurt you. Everyone is bending over backward to help you."

"I don't *want* anybody to help me. I don't *need* anybody. I don't like it here in this country," he yelled, "I hate school."

Grabbing at his arms, I tried to yank him off the staircase again; it was no use. In total frustration my anger turned to a burning rage, and I raised my hand to hit him. I wanted to hit him hard, but I caught myself and drew back. He didn't need to be hit.

I grabbed his arms once again and tried with all my might to pull him off the staircase, but he was too strong and had locked himself to it securely. By this time Tony was frenzied and I was livid.

He kept yelling, "I don't want any help. I can do it myself."

My inability to control Tony infuriated me. Before things got any worse and I lost my temper, I stood up, stepped over his body, and went up the stairs, turning to look down on him as I reached the landing.

His eyes flashed with hatred—at me, at everybody, at everything. "Tony, you're right. If you don't want my help there's nothing I can do for you."

Turning out the light, I went into my room and threw myself across the bed in utter despair. Feeling like a prisoner in my own home, I was tempted to get in my car and drive —drive anywhere—just get out of here! I wanted to be anyplace except home. It was Tony who'd been restricted, yet I was the one sitting in my room. When I finally went to bed physically and emotionally exhausted, I didn't even check on Tony.

As I dragged myself up the next morning, it was hard to open the door and face, not only another day, but Tony. What if he wasn't there? But where could he go? We were trapped —together!

His bedroom door was open. How could I be so angry with him yet so glad to see him? Apparently he had crawled up to bed sometime during the night and fallen asleep across his bed fully clothed. I sat down beside him on the bed and tried to smile. "I'm sorry about last night, Tony—sorry that we had to become so upset with each other."

He tried to answer but his voice stuttered and cracked and he sounded like a little baby. In fact, he acted very young and helpless. I couldn't believe this was the tough adolescent that had fought with me the night before. Now he wanted not only my help but also my love and affection, and especially my motherly reassurance.

Stroking his hair tenderly, I said, "Things are rough right now, Tony. I know they are, but I love you just the same. Even though I get angry or restrict you it's because I really love you with all my heart. I will never stop loving you. Now you remember that!"

It was a monumental task to get myself to work that morning, and I had to take Tony with me. I was still totally wrung out. My classes were increasingly hard to teach and my administrative tasks nearly overwhelmed me. It was a shock to realize how close to a breakdown I was coming.

That evening Tony managed to do his homework without too much complaint. However, he still talked like a baby, just as he had all day long.

About eight-thirty, I became a little nervous but steeled myself for whatever was to come, and at nine I turned off the television.

"Tony, it's time for bed," I announced. Tony looked at me in amazement. Was I actually going to follow through with the restriction that had devastated our relationship the night before?

Again, right before my eyes Tony turned from a cuddly little friend to a fierce, defiant brat. "You're not really going to make me, are you?" Even his voice sounded different, almost like a man's, and he grabbed onto the couch cushion.

"Yes, that's the restriction, sweets. You know it's going to last the rest of the week." For over six years in a prison Tony had been totally restricted. You would think he could handle a nine o'clock curfew.

"You won't let me do anything. You won't let me do anything!" Tony's voice rose in pitch and volume, rapidly moving into hysteria.

With a supreme effort, I forced myself to smile in an attempt to keep our conversation light. "You have lots of fun, but, right now, you are on restriction and you must go to bed at nine."

He seemed shocked that I was going to carry out my threat. "You can't do that," he yelled frantically. "You can't!"

What could I use to deal with defiance, rebellion, rage, and complete hysteria? Some people recommended a sound spanking. Did they realize that Tony had been nearly beaten to death several times during his short life? Others advised, "Restrict the boy and make sure you follow through with your discipline." Right then I wished my advisers were there with me to tell me how. In all our troubles we were sinking fast.

Communication, I thought. But it was very hard not to walk out the door and put it all off until tomorrow. I sat down beside Tony and tried to deal with this hideous "thing" that had come between us.

"The only reason that I'm here in the United States is because you *made* me come. This place is just like a prison."

I thought that my regular diet of trauma had toughened me, but Tony's words crushed me anew. Again, he was trying to manipulate me and I had to stand my ground.

"I need to ask you a very important question, Tony. Remember when you were still in La Granja? Lupe and the other lawyers came to visit you, and they told you that I wanted to be your mother. Do you remember what she asked you?" He looked down at his lap in silence. "She asked you if you would like to be my son and if you would like to come to live with me in the United States. Then she said to you, "Tony, 'Make sure that you really want to go with Carolyn before you say yes, because once you do, you will be her son forever.' Do you remember that, Tony?"

"Yes," he replied grudgingly.

"And what did you tell the lawyers, Tony?"

He refused to answer.

"You told them that you wanted to be my son. I'm glad you did, Tony, because I love you very much."

Tony quickly moved on to fresh battlegrounds. "Then the only reason that I'm here is because you make me stay! It's just like a prison!"

"Tony, look around our house. Do you see any bars on our windows? In a prison," I went on, "the locks are on the outside so that you cannot leave. Where are the locks in our house?"

He looked, "On the inside."

"That's right, Tony. You're not locked *in* this house and it is *not* a prison. This is your home. I will never *force* you to stay with me, but I *want* you to stay with me. You are my son and it will always be that way. You can't change that."

Our conversation had become quite serious, and we were both exhausted. By then we had used up most of the disputed hour discussing our relationship. So as I nudged him, he responded and followed me up the stairs. In silence I gave him a little hug, then we each went to our rooms, relieved that a major conflict had been avoided.

This week was threatening to become one of the longest in my life. I felt drained; I seemed to be doing all the giving in our relationship. When would Tony give me some of the things I craved—like love and respect. Of course, he had never received any love or respect in his entire life. How could I even dream that he would some day be able to give it? But I had dumped tons of love and respect into him already —what was he doing with all of it? Did he have an irreparable hole in his heart, so that everything that I put in fell out wasted? Was it hopeless?

I was asleep before my head hit the pillow.

Chapter Twenty-One

Tony's week and a half of restriction turned out to be a marathon of conflict that stripped away much of my zeal for life. But like a violent storm, when it was over, it was over, and our lives regained a semblance of normalcy.

"Normal" was too bland a description for our hot/cold, bitter/sweet, love/hate relationship. At that point in our lives there was no middle ground for us. When Tony was "good" we shared a magical happiness and camaraderie, but when he was "bad" our relationship fell through the middle ground of reason and compromise into an abyss filled with monstrous problems. But at least the "ups" seemed longer and the "downs" shorter.

But the biggest test was yet to come. Easter vacation was just a few weeks away and that meant we would be going to Mexicali with the university's Outreach team. Tony talked on and on about the guard Armando and how he took Tony home with him once in a while on his day off.

He remembered going to the show a couple of times with Armando's family and the wonderful freedom he had in Mexicali playing in the streets with Armando's children. From the way he talked about it, Mexicali sounded like paradise. He went on nostalgically about the "good ol' days," describing the neat ways that "real" Mexicans eat, play, and dress. And I had to agree that some things *were* different.

A couple of my close friends advised me not to take Tony to Mexicali this first year of our new relationship for fear that he might run away while there. Deep in my heart I knew the possibility was there. The last eight months had been hard on Tony, and he continually griped these days about the useless rules that Americans make up just to make life hard for people —especially little boys. He felt that adults were pushy, arrogant, and mean. It especially hurt me when he called our home a prison. So I felt the test could not be postponed; he needed that week back in Mexico.

Three or four days before the trip he altogether stopped talking about going. One night as we were having dinner I asked him directly, "Tony, how do you feel about going to Mexicali?"

His eyes finally rose to meet mine, "I don't know, Mom! I don't know!"

"Tony, do you want to go to Mexicali this year or would you rather have us stay home?"

For a few minutes he wrestled with his decision, then confirmed it. "No, I really want to go."

We drove to Mexicali with John and Barbara Fraley and their daughter, Jennifer. Tony was happy to see them again and chatted cheerfully all the way down. But when we crossed the border into Mexico, Tony became quiet; he was all eyes.

Mexican children scurried to the van when we stopped. With dirty rags in dirty little hands, they wiped at the dust on the car. When they held out their hands in hopes of payment, Tony spoke up from the backseat. "I used to do that," he said softly. More children approached and tried to sell us gum. Still others simply begged. Tony watched without comment, obviously recalling his own past.

For me, being in Mexicali lit the fires again under my sense of fun and adventure. When we turned in at the Cuernavaca mission, a thousand students were rapidly turning a dusty field into home for the week ahead.

Many had not yet heard about Tony being out of prison, so he caused a real uproar. He loved it. And for me, the cheerful greetings and affection from so many dear friends watered the core of my dry heart and brought forth springs of new life. I was on the verge of tears.

Forrest was there, already up to his elbows in dinner; Ron and Barb Cline had adopted a nine-year-old girl and would have some insights for me.

Tony really warmed up when he saw Grandma and

Grandpa Peters arrive with their team from Twain Harte. No one could believe how well he spoke English. It was new for Tony to be there as part of the team rather than in the prison being visited by the team. Danny Barker hugged and teased Tony and played the piano for him anytime Tony wanted.

"Hey Tony, I'm going to play for the team at La Granja in a few days. Do you want to go with me?"

"Sure!" he lit up.

"Great, Tony. But you better ask your Mom first."

Back at the "Little Hilton" I was busy getting our stuff in order when Tony burst in.

"Hi, sweets, and how do you like camp?"

"A lot. I have lots of friends here." He paused, "Mom, can I go to La Granja with Danny? He said I could."

"That depends," I paused, "Do you *want* to go?"

"Yeah, maybe we'll see Armando."

"Okay, Tony, tell Danny that you can go, but I want to go along!"

As camp director, I was kept busy with many administrative tasks. So I sent Tony out to the villages with his grandparents, the Peterses, to give him a break from me. That evening Alva told me, "Tony wouldn't participate today in the games and crafts."

"That's not like him," I said. "Do you think he's sick?"

"No, not at all," Alva replied thoughtfully. "He just sat there staring a hole through the Mexican children. He acts as though he's doing some serious thinking."

The day before Tony was to go to La Granja, he sought me out when he knew I'd be alone in the trailer. It didn't take long to realize that he had something on his mind, although it took several minutes of fiddling with my clipboard and pencil for him to work up to it.

"Mom?"

Well, that was a beginning.

"Yes, Tony?"

"Mom," he paused, "Do I *have* to go to La Granja?"

"Of course not, honey."

"I don't think I want to go, Mom."

"Tony, you never have to go back to La Granja as long as you live." I wasn't surprised that he wasn't ready to face that memory just yet. Being in Mexico for a week must be overwhelming enough.

Since Tony avoided even the local market at home because of all the people, I was surprised to see him fit in so well at camp. Instead of retreating to the trailer, overwhelmed by a thousand people, he joined in and helped with chores and thoroughly enjoyed everyone. During several staff meetings he came in and seated his skinny little body on my lap. "This is *my* chair," he would announce.

On the last day of camp Tony and I sat in the Little Hilton for a long talk. I wanted to hear his impressions of the week.

"I had lots of fun." His first response was very cheerful, but then he sat back in his chair and became thoughtful.

"What is it, Tony?"

"Well, Mom," he paused for quite a long moment, "it's very dirty here, isn't it?"

Inside I wanted to laugh; I had suspected all along that Tony had romanticized life in Mexicali. "Yes, honey, it *is* dirty. These are good and decent people here, but they don't have nearly as much as we do in the United States."

"I guess I'm really lucky, aren't I, Mom?" We both grinned.

"I guess I'm really lucky, too; I have you. God has worked a real miracle in our lives, hasn't he?"

"Yeah." And Tony reached out and wrapped his arms around me.

The drive through Mexicali to the border had a new significance for Tony this time. He had chosen to be Tony Koons and was leaving Mexico for good.

At the border, there was a long line of cars as usual, and I told Tony to get out his green card. As we got closer to the crossing, the alarm on Tony's face was unmistakable.

"It's okay, Tony," I reassured him. "They'll let you out; just show your green card."

He wanted to believe me but couldn't quite. As we pulled up before the border guard, I looked back at Tony. He had plastered his green card right to his nose and was peering over the top like a frightened pup.

"Are you all American citizens?" the guard asked.

"Yes," we each responded. "And this is my son, Tony. He was born in Mexico."

The guard reached in and took Tony's card. Tony froze. The guard looked at the card, then at Tony, then back at the card. With a smile he returned it and waved us through the border.

Tony sighed in relief and turned to wave at the guard.

That week in Mexicali made a big difference in Tony. He felt that he belonged with me, and seemed very comfortable with his decision. He also seemed more a part of the community; he became involved with the young people at Glenkirk Presbyterian Church and planned to attend a weekend camp in the mountains nearby. I was jubilant! How many good restaurants could I eat at in two short days? This would be our first time apart since he had come to the United States, and I intended to make the most of it.

Tony made the most of it, too—hiking, crafts, mischief with flashlights after lights out—all the normal kinds of things he had never done before.

Best of all was his new friend. Ted was a tall, skinny boy of part Mexican descent. He was not only Tony's age but adopted, too. After being abandoned in downtown Los Angeles by his mother as an infant, the Torres family had adopted him.

With the Mexicali trip, camp, and a new friend to bolster his morale, Tony actually showed signs of putting some effort into his last month of school. And before we knew it, school was finally out.

One day, at the beginning of the summer, I had a long talk with Tony about all that had happened at school.

"This year was really rough. Well, at least it was for me. How was it for you, Tony?"

"Rough," he admitted with a grin.

I couldn't help smiling. I was proud of him. It had been his first experience with education—in two different schools in two different grades in a new country with a new language; he even had a new mom. He had begun to shift away from his emphasis on survival. Beneath all the toughness of my son and all the garbage that he dragged around from his past, there was a beautiful, exciting, charismatic young man, bursting to get free. I could often see this special inner person in his eyes.

Even with the pressures of school over for a while, Tony still preferred to be a hermit. Only during his twice-weekly Little League practices could I sneak off to the market. Every Saturday he had a game. As soon as Little League ended, I would have to plan some outings for us.

Ted was a real help, coaxing Tony out to ride bicycles all over town. Ted was quite adventuresome, and sometimes they'd be gone quite a long time. If they were gone for more than a couple of hours, though, Tony would telephone home to check on me. Deep inside he must still have harbored the fear that I would leave him.

Tony was addicted to television. As an educator this really alarmed me; unfortunately Tony had heard one of his teachers tell me that watching would help him learn English faster. His argument for "one more show" soon wore thin. "But Mom, I'm learning English this way," he would grin.

One evening while I studied at my desk, Tony entertained himself with his favorite program, a police show. About halfway through, something happened.

"Mom, Mom," Tony called in alarm. "Come here, quick!"

His alarm was contagious, so I hurried in. He jabbed at the screen. "Look, Mom! Look at him!" He grabbed my arm, "Look, Mom, he's alive."

"What are you talking about, Tony?"

"Look at that man," he ran to the television and pointed

to the man, then ran back to me and just about shook my arm off. "Mom, that man is alive!"

"Tony, all those people are alive."

"No! You don't understand! He was killed last night. I saw it on TV!"

Amazed and amused, I tried to reassure him. "Tony, he's just acting. This is just a story, it's not for real."

"No, Mom," he insisted. "It *is* for real. I even saw the blood and they buried him in the ground and some people cried."

"Do you believe that all the pictures you watch on television are true?"

"Yes."

I couldn't believe my ears. "Tony, these people are only acting out these stories. It's a job for them. After the program is over, they go home to their real families."

"Well, he didn't go home last night," Tony argued, "because he was dead! How can he be alive tonight?"

"Do you understand what it means to be an actor?"

He looked at me, very bewildered, and said no.

I tried to explain television and acting to him, but he seemed confused and not only rejected but resented my insinuations about his heroes. This situation called for outside help, so that Saturday, Ted, Tony, and I made a special trip to Universal Studios. Tony was alternately speechless and brimming with questions as he watched someone fall from a high building to a bloody death then stand up and take a bow. We watched airplanes crash and buildings collapse in make-believe earthquakes. And the whole day, to Tony's delight, we were surrounded by costumed actors. The complex machinery and photographic tricks that gave the Bionic Man his superhuman powers were explained to us.

Other than his disillusionment at the Bionic Man's "deception," Tony enjoyed the excursion immensely (though he rather lost his zeal for our Bionic Mom game). At one point, a mechanical shark jumped out of the water and came within inches of Ted. When he screamed and jumped back, Tony and I laughed and laughed.

Several weeks later, as Ted and Tony and I were enjoying a television program, one of the characters was shot and fell over dead.

"You know, Ted," he said confidently, "they aren't really dead, they're just pretending."

Then hesitantly he turned his head toward me, "They *are* pretending, aren't they, Mom?"

It wasn't long before we made a second trip to Universal Studios.

Socially as well as academically, Tony had some catching up to do. Because he had been around men and boys almost exclusively, girls were a real novelty. To make matters worse, he was galloping into adolescence faster than I could cover all the childhood bases he had missed. So at a social level much lower than his physical maturity, Tony became girl crazy. He was too shy to approach them, but he and Ted loved to talk about them. Friends assured me that this was very normal behavior, but I still worried: the topic seemed to occupy about 95 percent of their conversation!

With time, however, the boys gained more confidence. If we went somewhere and they became interested in a girl, they would ingeniously figure out how to get her phone number. At home again, it would take only minutes for Tony to get on the phone and happily stutter his way through a conversation.

Our bedtime talks soon shifted to conversations about girls. His honesty was very refreshing, and I took full advantage of this opportunity to teach him how to relate to females. I wasn't always in time to help him avoid a social blunder, but he did seem to appreciate my counsel anyway.

Girls were always a high priority, but we had to deal with a few other ethics—like work! It was a never-ending source of conflict, and it was quite some time before I could recognize why.

One cause was Tony's definite but highly distorted image of the Mexican work ethic for males. My first clue came one afternoon; I was studying, and Tony called to me from the living room.

"Mom, come here!"

"What do you want?"

"Come here," he demanded.

"I'm studying, Tony. Please come in here."

"No," he yelled, "I need you in here."

"This had better be good, Tony. I'm right in the middle of something."

He was reclined on the couch, his head resting on several pillows, watching television.

"What do you want?"

He gestured imperially toward the set. "Change the channel for me," he commanded.

What gall! My saber-sharp stare punctured Tony's puffed up importance. Then I snapped off the television set and leaned against it with my arms crossed and continued to stare at him. It wasn't long before he dropped his head sheepishly.

"I don't know just where you got the idea that a mother is a slave," I began, "but let me make myself very clear, Tony. I am *not* your slave." I paused carefully to let my statement have its effect. "Don't *ever* call me to change the channel for you again, or I'll turn it off and it will stay off!"

Early on, Tony had made it clear that he shouldn't have to help me in the kitchen. "Mexican men don't work in the kitchen. They watch TV while the women work." Or, "Mexican boys play in the street and the girls help their mothers in the house." He even tried to convince me that Mexican men didn't work *at all!* I'm sure this would have come as a real surprise to a lot of hard-working Mexican men. But where had Tony developed these attitudes? He hadn't been in any Mexican homes except Armando's since he was five.

It would be a big adjustment for Tony to realize that work was good and healthy for his soul.

Another conflict over work came whenever I asked Tony

to do anything more than his regular chores, no matter how small. These he handled very well—he kept his bed made and his room neat, took out the trash every Wednesday, and cleared the table and loaded the dishwasher after each meal.

But occasionally our garage needed a little extra cleaning, especially after Tony finished one of his building projects or bike-repair extravaganzas. I would warn him that in several days he would need to do that job. He would agree. But when Saturday rolled around, he would absolutely refuse to do it.

"You don't love me, you hate me," he would yell. "What did I ever do to you?"

How could such a simple chore evoke such a strong response? With the energy he wasted fighting about it, he could have cleaned the whole garage many times over. "Mom, what did I do to you!?" he would say. Finally, when I gave in and offered to help he would grudgingly work with me. But the minute I left, he would quit.

We have a tiny, eight-foot section of grass in our backyard that needs weeding periodically. As was my habit, I gave him several days warning (I knew he hated surprises), then one evening took him outside and showed him what I expected. I told him that the job should take only thirty minutes.

"I would appreciate your help so much, Tony; it would really help me. I have a lot of cleaning to do in the house."

As I left, he started in at me. "What did I do to you? Why do you hate me!?"

His response didn't make any sense at all. In fact, it made me angry. After all, didn't I do an awful lot of work for him? So, I insisted that he do the work. Four hours later, well into darkness, he sat there fuming and seething—not having pulled a single weed.

Finally, around ten, he asked, "Can I come in now?" He was quiet but not in the least contrite.

"Yes, Tony, but go on up to bed."

"Can I watch television?"

"No, son, the television will not go on until the weeds are pulled. It can take you thirty minutes or thirty years, but the television stays off until the weeds are pulled."

He went on up to his room. "Why do you hate me so much?" he yelled down the stairs, "Why do you hate me?"

That night, too confused to sleep, I puzzled over his behavior. What makes him think that I hate him just because I ask for his help in our home? Then scenes from La Granja flashed into my mind. All the boys had regular chores but anyone who misbehaved was assigned extra chores as punishment.

That was it. Tony felt he was being punished each time I asked him to do any extra work. My frustration was relieved but the problem remained—how to teach Tony a healthy respect for a good day's work. For him work was punishment. Right then, Tony could have benefitted from a strong male role model, but I was too withdrawn to ask for help. I just wanted someone to appear and volunteer to love Tony and teach him about being a man.

My friend Jim Slevcov owned a Christian camp near Yosemite. For three weeks each summer there was backpacking, water skiing, and sailing, all with a Christian emphasis. Several of our Mexicali Outreach staff members were working there this summer. I had worked in camps myself, and I knew that the experience would be good for Tony, so I talked it over with him and he reluctantly consented to go.

Just before camp started we spent several days with the Peterses, and Grandma Alva joined us for the drive to Yosemite. By this time, Tony was digging his heels in. "Mom, I don't want to go," he almost cried. "Do I have to go?"

"Tony, don't forget that Sammy and Randy from the Mexicali staff will be there. You'll have a wonderful time, honey!"

But, deep inside I had begun to have my own misgivings. Tony and I had been inseparable for over a year now and it would be hard to be away from him. How strange: I had looked forward so eagerly to some time by myself; now the thought of being away from him for three weeks bothered me.

"Please don't make me go," Tony continued to beg. His reluctance seemed to be escalating into panic. He looked into my eyes and said, "Mom, will you be there when camp is over?"

"Yes, Tony, I'll be waiting for you. When you get home we'll hug and sit down at the kitchen table and talk all about it. You know something, Tony? I'm going to miss you very much!"

The camp, on the shores of Bass Lake, was gorgeous. We headed for a large central building in the middle, the meeting place for campers and their parents. It seemed like old home week for Alva and me since we knew Jim and Manya Slevcov and many of the staff, but Tony was withdrawn and sullen.

When it was time for the parents to leave I hugged and kissed Tony. "I love you, son. Look for my letters and I will see you in three weeks."

I had hoped that having Sammy there would ease our separation; he and Tony had been such pals in Mexicali. But Tony turned to Alva.

"Grandma," he begged frantically, "Don't let her leave me. Please, Grandma, don't let her leave me here!"

His words pierced my soul; only the cruelest mother in the world could abandon such a terrified son. It was awful, but I managed to tear myself away. I could see him in the rearview mirror still frantically yelling, "Don't leave me, don't leave me!"

I fought back my own tears. All the way back to Alva's I couldn't get Tony's pathetic little face out of my mind. Depression moved in solidly.

"He'll be fine, Carolyn," Alva comforted. "They'll keep him so busy doing new things that he won't have time to even think about you. And besides, he needs to learn that he can trust you."

"I wish he would!"

"Well, anyway, Carolyn, this separation will be good for you. It's been a long year."

Soothing though Alva's words may have been, the memory of Tony's distress kept drowning them out.

The next three weeks were a crazy mixture of relief and exhaustion. For the first time in over a year I didn't have to coerce Tony into doing his chores, talk him out of bed in the morning, threaten him into bed at night, coax him from the television set to the dinner table, or question whether he had had a bath! I was completely free to do whatever sounded good to me. And do you know what sounded best? Calling Tony. I wanted so badly to know how he was getting along. But it was best for everyone if I let him have these weeks to himself. Sammy, Jim, the director, and his wife were all committed to making camp a wonderful experience for Tony.

Tony had told me that he became a Christian while he was in La Granja, but he suffered with so many doubts that I prayed about it daily for him. Being away from me and away from all his problems might give him an opportunity to be alone with God.

Tony still believed that God shouldn't allow him to do so many bad things. Over and over I tried to explain to him that God wants our love and obedience on a voluntary basis only. But these were things that Tony had to work out for himself.

Praying to God for a healing in memory was something that I embraced strongly, not only for myself, but for others. The emotional wounds out of Tony's past bled all over everything he did, so I continued to pray. With a group of people from Russ and Alva's church one Saturday morning, I prayed quite some time about each aspect of Tony's past. We asked God to heal his memory and release him to become all that God intended—the fears, angers, and frustrations, we prayed for them all!

When the camp car full of laughing boys pulled up in front of the house, Tony flew out and around the corner of the house, yelling, "Mom, Mom, I'm home!" I met him halfway down the walk with a hug from the heart of a hungry mother.

The very next thing that Tony said was, "Can I go back

next year, Mom? I had a great time. I loved it. Can I go back, huh, Mom?"

Randy came up behind him. "He had a wonderful time, Carolyn, and he loved every minute."

I squeezed Tony tightly, "I knew you would, babe."

I invited Randy to stay for dinner. Tony couldn't stop talking about camp. He told me about his backpacking trip and the heavy pack that he had carried and then described in detail actually climbing the back side of Half Dome in Yosemite. He went on forever about his buddies in the dorm and he was so cute when he giggled about the costume party they had one night.

Randy managed to get a word in: "Tony was a very popular guy around camp. Everyone was drawn to him because he was so alive and happy." He chuckled a little under his breath.

"What's so funny?"

"Just—Tony's nickname, Moo-Cow!" Randy laughed.

"Moo-Cow? You're kidding!"

"Yeah, Mom, that's right," Tony boasted, "my name was Moo-Cow."

"Why in the world did they call you that, Tony?"

Before my question was out, I knew the answer. Tony cupped his hands around his mouth and his eyes danced with anticipation as a horrendous bellow that sounded exactly like a cow, a big cow, came roaring out of his mouth. It was the biggest moo that I had heard since my days on the farm in Minnesota. How good it was to be laughing with my son, the old shadows of trouble never darkening his face.

I was happier still to learn that Tony had found time to be with God and had surrendered his life to Jesus Christ. He told me that Jesus was going to help him this next year.

I thanked God for answering our prayers.

Chapter Twenty-Two

As a rule I wear optimism as easily as a zebra does stripes; I was born a survivor. Some people interpret my attitude as a need to be independent, to "make it on my own," but it's far from that! God planted within me a desire to "be a winner," to "succeed," and I've carefully nurtured that desire.

Looking back over my first year with Tony I freely admitted that it was hell on earth two out of every three days. But beneath his tough skin, Tony was a great kid; we were going to have a good second year. Optimistic people don't deny problems; they simply find a way to make their problems work for them. We would use all that we had learned last year toward making this year better. Or so I reasoned!

As our second September rolled around, Tony didn't seem to mind going back to school. He loved seeing Mrs. Spurling again, even if she did send homework home.

Early that first week, Tony came crashing in through the front door. "Mom, Mom," he yelled, "they're starting a basketball team at school. Can I play?"

"Whoa, boy! Why don't you tell me a little bit about it?"

"You know, Mom, like soccer, we'll have practice after school, then games once a week. And we have to buy a uniform, too. A new teacher named Mr. Lantz is going to be the coach. Can I play?"

"Sure Tony, it will be good for you. I'll be happy to have you play. But remember, you still have to do your homework and a half hour of reading at night."

For the first several days of practice Tony was very excited about being on the team, and bragged a lot about being a good player. Maybe he was behaving like a hot shot, but the other players would soon rub those edges off!

It didn't seem to bother Tony when the team lost their first game; he just loved playing. So I was surprised when he came to me rather upset just before the second game.

"Mom, I want to quit the basketball team."

"But why? I thought you really liked it."

"I just want to quit," he insisted.

"You need to have a good reason to quit the team, Tony. What if everyone up and quit?"

"I just want to quit, that's all."

Well, I had never been a quitter in my life so I encouraged him to stick with the team. But my daily enthusiasm did little to bolster Tony's spirits. They lost the second game, too, and he became almost sullen. The third was finally a home game, so I went to watch.

The junior high cheerleaders looked very cute and did a good job of rousing team spirit in the crowded stands. Even Mr. Cook, the principal, was there to cheer at the first home game. Soon, Coach Lantz and the team charged onto the court and began some pregame warm-ups. The coach yelled instructions from the sidelines. He was a short man in his thirties with an unusually red face. I tried to tell myself that he was energetic—but that wasn't it. He appeared nervous and angry!

Within seconds the other team scored, and Mr. Lantz bolted off the bench and berated his own team. "You idiots!" he yelled. "What a bunch of clumsy fools!" The stands became quiet except for a few derogatory remarks about the coach. Mr. Lantz beat a towel into his hand and began to look almost deranged. "Come on, you idiots," he yelled again, "get that ball!"

By now the team was thoroughly befuddled by his undisciplined behavior and fumbled the ball miserably. They missed their first shot at the basket by two feet, and Mr. Lantz came completely unglued. He ran down to the basket and screamed, "Why don't you watch the ball! Now, get that ball, would you!" The other team starting snickering at him; he *did* seem ridiculously angry.

Sliding down the bench toward Mr. Cook, I asked, "Did you notice the coach yelling at our team?"

He looked at me in some embarrassment, "Yes I did, Carolyn. I'm going to have to speak with him."

The team lost by fifteen points, and I drove my distraught son home.

"Mom, Mr. Lantz yells all the time and makes me embarrassed at our games. Can't you make him stop yelling?"

"Tony, he does yell; he behaves very immaturely. In fact, I was embarrassed by it. He's wrong to act that way, Tony. But unfortunately, you're going to have people yelling at you the rest of your life; the world is full of immature people. I wish you could be protected from all the yelling you'll have to face, but I can't possibly run around making them stop. You're going to have to learn to live with it. Do you understand?"

"But he makes me mad!"

"Try not to let him get to you. Just remember, if you fight back or yell back, you're showing you're as immature as he is."

"Mom?"

"Yes, Tony."

"Mr. Lantz is also the seventh-grade history teacher."

A red flag. We were headed for trouble.

Throughout the semester I had kept close tabs on Tony through Mrs. Spurling. He was reading at a third-grade level, which was just fine, considering that he was in only his second year of school. He was seeing a speech therapist for his stuttering, but it was still too soon to expect results. (I wasn't terribly concerned; I believed that when Tony finally worked through his other problems, the stuttering would take care of itself.)

One day well into the semester, she said, "Tony seems to have lost his spark lately."

I agreed. "He's been very quiet at home these last few weeks. That's usually an indication that something is building up somewhere else in his life—like at school."

"He just doesn't seem as happy as usual. He's special, Carolyn, and I love him very much." She winked and gave me a little nudge. "Tony and I understand each other, you know! Tony's problem lately might be that he and Mr. Lantz aren't getting along. Mr. Lantz seems to be developing a reputation as a yeller, and you know how Tony reacts to that. Why don't you go talk with Mr. Cook?''

Mr. Cook had good things to say about Tony's development both socially and academically.

I brought up the tension between Tony and Mr. Lantz. "Have you ever confronted the coach about the way he yells?''

"Well, I've mentioned it," he confessed. "He's new to teaching and has a lot to learn, but I plan to speak to him again.''

Changing Lantz was going to take longer than I had hoped. Toward the end of the basketball season, Lantz went into a tirade at the boys for missing the basket too many times. Tony stood up for the team and exploded at the rampaging teacher. He was kicked off the team and sent to the principal's office. Later—as usual—I found out that Tony had been sent to the office several times for yelling back at Mr. Lantz.

When I confronted Tony about his behavior he was indignant. "I don't understand," he complained, "why Mr. Lantz doesn't get into trouble for yelling at us. He yells a lot more than I do.''

"Tony, I agree that Mr. Lantz's behavior is not right, but that's between him and Mr. Cook. Right now, it seems that you have developed a yelling problem of your own.''

"I just can't stand it when he yells at us, so I tell him.''

"You mean, you scream at him," I corrected.

"He makes me mad!'' Tony fumed through his teeth.

"Tony, you're responsible for how you respond to Mr. Lantz whether you like what he says or not. Just because he makes you angry doesn't mean that you can yell at him! Do you agree?''

He nodded outwardly but I knew that on the inside he was still very angry. In a way Tony's yelling back was almost therapeutic—but at the same time, it was definitely wrong and couldn't be encouraged.

Some things just naturally fall into a sequence: thunder and lightning, smoke and fire, boasting and disaster.

I was sitting out in my secretary's office expounding on Tony's improvement at school. (You'd think I'd know better by now.) Just then the phone rang. Sonja answered it, responded briefly, and hung up. "Mr. Cook would like to see you. Tony has been suspended from school!" My barely inflated heart sank—glub, blub, right to the bottom.

I walked past Tony and the school secretary directly into Mr. Cook's office. It was hard to tell whether Tony looked hurt or confused, but if this was a typical situation he was probably both.

I forced myself to ask the dreaded question: "What happened?"

"Mr. Lantz's class got a little out of control today, so after several warnings he told them to 'shut-up' and take out a piece of paper and write fifty times, 'I will not talk in Mr. Lantz's class.' Everyone took out a piece of paper, Carolyn, except Tony."

"What did he do?" I hardly dared to ask.

"According to Lantz, and Tony agrees, he flew out of his chair and said, with that defiant tone he uses, 'You make me!' "

About that time I was ready to sew Tony's lips shut. "What did Mr. Lantz do then?"

"He ordered Tony to sit down. He refused. Lantz tried to grab him but Tony was too quick for him and jumped out of the way. When Tony started laughing at him, Lantz became even more angry and grabbed at Tony again. This time Tony jumped on top of a desk and started leaping from one desk top to another all over the room.

"Mr. Lantz made one foolish attempt after another to catch Tony, until the whole class was laughing at him. Finally, he yelled at Tony to get out of his room and down to my office, and that he was suspended. And I heard every word of it clear down here," Cook sighed.

"He did leave then, didn't he?" I asked, praying at the same time.

"Oh yes, he came to my office," Mr. Cook shook his head

in disbelief, "but first he grinned at Lantz triumphantly and strutted out the door! I'm sorry, Carolyn, but Tony will be suspended for the remainder of this week and all of next!"

They should have had a record made: "I'm sorry, Carolyn, Tony will be suspended . . . I'm sorry, Carolyn, Tony will be suspended . . . I'm sorry . . ."

"I'm sorry, too, Mr. Cook! Couldn't this have been avoided? Haven't you talked to Mr. Lantz about his yelling?"

"Yes, but apparently it hasn't done any good. Both you and Mrs. Spurling warned me that this would happen. Really, I do hate to do this, Carolyn, but Mr. Lantz is totally unglued at this point."

"That makes several of us, doesn't it?"

Tony and I drove home in silence, then automatically gravitated to the couch. "All right Tony, tell me what happened."

To my surprise, he repeated Mr. Cook's rendition almost verbatim.

"You mean that you actually did jump from desk to desk?"

"Yes," he answered emphatically, but without a trace of arrogance.

"Tony, were you right or wrong?"

"I was wrong," he admitted, slightly embarrassed but not hesitating.

"I don't get it, Tony; if you knew it was wrong, why did you do it?"

He looked me straight in the eyes, "Mom, Mr. Lantz told us to write something fifty times, and he didn't even write it on the board for us to copy. I don't know how to write that stuff. I don't want the kids in that school to know I can't write, because they'll think that I'm stupid." Tony was determined as he leaned forward on the couch toward me, "*And I am not stupid!* I'd rather get kicked out of school than have the kids think I'm stupid." He folded his arms and put on the triumphant look he must have used on Mr. Lantz. "So, I won!"

It was impossible to argue with his logic, but we certainly

discussed the benefit of some constructive alternative solutions to his dilemma for future reference.

The next day I stopped in to see Mr. Lantz, not to defend Tony, but to clear up a few things.

When I explained why Tony had reacted the way he did, Mr. Lantz looked shocked.

"Didn't you know that writing was difficult for Tony?"

"No." He looked mortified at my question.

It was beyond me how he could have Tony in his history class for months and not know he couldn't write. I took a deep breath and continued, "Mr. Lantz, are you aware that you yell at your students?"

He looked at the floor. "Yes, Miss Koons. I'm trying hard to stop; I'm very sorry. Mr. Cook talked with me yesterday. I'm sorry about Tony. We'll get him back in class right away, okay?"

"No, we've worked out his lessons with Mrs. Spurling, and he'll manage fine at home. This punishment is justified because Tony knew exactly what he was doing. But he does need to learn that yelling doesn't solve anything."

Mr. Lantz looked embarrassed.

Tony returned to school, but the cease-fire didn't last. By the third day they had declared war against each other. Koons versus Lantz, or Lantz versus Koons—regardless of who had fired the first shot, it was now mutual.

A couple of weeks later, Tony came home seething about something. He threw his books on the floor and crashed into the chair.

"Mr. Lantz thinks I'm bad!"

"What?"

"Mr. Lantz said that I'm no good. He said that I'm bad and that there's nothing good in me!" Tony was furious, and he said it again, "He thinks that I'm bad so I'll show him! I'll be bad, real bad! He doesn't know what bad is!"

Tony's declaration brought back vividly a shockingly similar experience from my own past. I had made the same decision and lived to regret it. I had been careful to build Tony's self-image against this very attitude. Now Mr. Lantz was tearing it down.

I decided to keep a close eye on the situation, so I picked Tony up every day after school and even arrived early to see his basketball practice. I was surprised he stayed on the team. The cold war between Tony and his coach was undisguised: Tony was insolent; Mr. Lantz was unjust. If the team lined up, he would pull Tony out of the middle and put him at the end. If they practiced shooting, Tony was relegated to catching balls and never shooting one. During the other drills Lantz singled Tony out and yelled at him continually. After practice Tony was assigned to put the balls away. I felt miserable watching the struggle between the two of them.

Within days came the inevitable phone call and there I was, sitting again in the principal's office listening to my son's latest escapade.

"Tony was sitting with a group of boys around the lunch table this noon," Mr. Cook began, "when one of them pulled a cupcake from his lunch. Before he could unwrap it another kid at the table grabbed it and passed it to the boy next to him. You know how boys like to tease. Naturally, everyone became involved as they passed the cupcake just out of the owner's reach. When he started screaming, Mr. Lantz, who was on lunch duty, went to investigate. As he approached, the cupcake was thrown to Tony, who taunted the boy by holding it at arm's length."

Mr. Cook continued telling the story without comment. "Mr. Lantz was infuriated and started screaming at Tony, accusing him of stealing the cupcake and starting the whole incident. Tony denied it, and the other boys came to his defense. That made Lantz madder still. He continued to scream accusations at Tony, but Tony stood his ground and denied them. With all the boys yelling in Tony's defense, Mr. Lantz lost control, grabbed him by the neck, and wrenched him backward off the bench. Tony went crazy; he jumped up, reached into his pocket and pulled out a knife, and pointed it at Lantz." Red welts around Tony's neck indicated where Lantz had grabbed him. "Tony's neck had been badly bruised, and he wasn't going to give Lantz another chance at it."

Mr. Cook continued, "At first Lantz just stared at the knife; then he started yelling for the other teachers to come help him. The other boys tried to grab the knife from Tony, but he panicked and turned it on them. Lantz saw his chance and went for Tony's neck again; he threw him to the ground and kicked the knife out of his hand. Then he dragged him in here to me."

I sat there speechless. What could I say? My whole world was collapsing around me. A knife! All I wanted to do was run and scream myself. I wasn't ready to handle a problem like this.

"It's awful!" I finally said, exhausted. "Tony was wrong. There is no excuse whatsoever for his pulling a knife. But Mr. Cook, what are you going to do about that teacher?"

"The school board is meeting to determine his future here at the school. Tony isn't the only one who has had problems with him, Carolyn. But that doesn't get Tony off the hook," Mr. Cook warned. "He didn't steal the cupcake or even start the commotion, but, Carolyn, he went berserk and pulled a knife. I should kick him out of school—for good—but because of the circumstances and because he was probably provoked by a teacher, I'm going to suspend him for two weeks instead."

The marks remained on Tony's neck for well over a week. He felt blamed for starting the cupcake fight and saw pulling the knife as pure self-defense. Exasperated and weary, he looked at me and said, "If everyone thinks I'm so bad, I guess I am!"

Chapter Twenty-Three

By the grace of God, both Tony and I had lived through my first year of motherhood. But the horror of that year had far exceeded my worst expectations. Sure, there had been lots of good times, but right now they were about as easy for me to remember as my grandmother, whom I'd only met once.

I have always believed that if I wanted something badly enough and worked very hard to get it, I would succeed. But now, any time day or night that I dared to look up, the buzzards of failure were circling. The sight of them so sickened me that I was afraid to look up anymore.

Tony's decision to prove that he was as "bad" as everyone thought he was came from the core of his soul. He chose to push God aside and allow his heart to become a cesspool of confusion and anger.

During the summer Tony's behavior had looked so promising that I was actually looking forward to our second year. But as the year wore on I realized that he was like a delicate plant that only did well in the perfect conditions of a hothouse. School was definitely not a "hothouse" for Tony.

I watched for progress in Tony's behavior, but I had to admit that he was regressing. In fact, things were becoming more explosive daily. Tony had started out by hitting his teacher, then he had begun using the karate kick, and now he'd progressed to pulling a knife. He was still reacting just as though he were in La Granja. La Granja wasn't almost two years behind us—it was today!

Pulling a knife on someone was serious, so along with the suspension, Tony had further restrictions, one of which was to stay home during school hours (or, when necessary, accompany me down to the university). And the other was a nine o'clock curfew. Only by a supreme effort could I enforce the curfew; I felt I was losing my grip as the pendulum of control swung in Tony's direction.

At bedtime I wanted to call the National Guard to help me. Some nights he fought me for hours, but I persisted; he never watched even a minute's worth of television after nine. But it was getting so I had to talk myself into crawling out of bed in the morning. Why bother? I thought.

One morning, after an especially difficult bedtime struggle the night before, I called Alva, then Happy and Jerry. While Tony watched television, I sought advice and encouragement. The night restriction was the big issue, I explained. Tony hated going to bed—no matter what the time.

"You've got to stick it out, Carolyn," they encouraged. "This is a crucial time."

I was beginning to think that *all* of our time together was crucial! When would it let up? It was nearly impossible to accomplish anything at work with Tony hanging around the office, so I gave up my office hours during his suspension and worked at home until class time.

"Tony, I'm going to dash down to the school and teach my class, then come straight home. I want you to stay here. You may play in the house, the patio, or the garage, but *do not leave.* All the kids are still in school until three; you can go out and play then. Do you understand?"

"Yes," he agreed.

"You *do* understand that I want you to stay here?"

"Yes, Mom."

"Okay, Tony, I'll see you in a little over an hour—about two."

Upon returning home, the first thing I noticed was that Tony's bike was missing. I checked in the house and didn't find him. I drove to his old school, but he wasn't there; to the park, through the streets of Glendora—no Tony. I drove back home, then down to Donny's and back home again, over to the park—still no Tony! For an hour I looked but couldn't find him. My body was bone tired, but I grew angrier by the minute. He was defying my authority.

An hour and a half later, Tony strolled in with a lordly sneer on his impudent face.

Restrictions didn't work; reasoning with him didn't work. Spending more and more time with him or forcing him to bed or even pleading with him simply did not make him obey me. The only thing I hadn't tried was a spanking. Maybe that's what he really wanted.

"Tony, go to your room!"

Now, nobody had ever taught me how to spank a child. If I used my hand, I'd probably hurt *it,* but a leather belt might really hurt *him.* What I want to do is just sting the back of his legs a bit, I reasoned. So I grabbed the fly swatter. It didn't look too lethal, but I figured it would do the job. As I walked into his room, Tony gave me an insolent glare, challenging me to take him on.

"Tony, I've tried everything I know of to deal with your misbehavior. Now I'm going to do what every parent must do on occasion. I am going to spank you."

When I reached for his arm to turn him around, he flew into action. Before I realized what he was doing, his foot shot up in his now-infamous karate kick and landed squarely on the side of my head. I felt like I'd been kicked by a horse. I fell back against the closet door and slid partway to the floor, giving Tony ample time to recover his stance and crouch ominously for a second round. Who did this kid think he was, anyway? I'm from the streets, too! I rushed him, ducking his karate kick, and threw him on the floor, able to pin him with my larger body. We lay there on the floor—I had one arm across his neck, my legs over his to keep him from kicking, and my right arm holding his hands down to keep him from hitting me; he, sure that I was going to kill him, fought with all his might to save his life. Anger and panic were reflected in his eyes; had Mom become another Senor Manuel? I, in turn, appalled at finding myself in a physical fight with my thirteen-year-old son, began thinking "mother" should be spelled in blood. We both lay there struggling for what seemed like hours.

Finally, I felt his body go limp with exhaustion. Knowing

he wouldn't kick me now, I released him and walked out of his room into mine, slamming my door behind me. I didn't want to even be near Tony.

If things had been bad before, it was nothing compared with how they were now. Tony was "bad" and bad people didn't smile or talk very much at all; most important, bad people did not obey.

Tony discovered manipulation; he did his chores only when he wanted something. It was pretty effective, too. Forced to fight him tooth and nail about everything, I was thrilled when he showed the least sign of compliance and would usually grant his request. He no longer made his bed or kept his room in order—unless there was something in it for him—and he defied everything I said.

We were able to move from one day to the next only because I never let Tony know that he was getting to me. I gritted my teeth so hard that they ached; in fact, my whole body ached. I could hardly wait to get into bed at night, but bedtime was usually delayed until quite late because Tony would pitch a fit and refuse to go.

I would fall into bed each night too tired even to snuggle in and get comfortable; it was too much effort. No sooner would I fall asleep than Tony would quietly open my door and hiss, "You can't make me do anything." Over and over and over he would taunt me, "I won't obey you. I won't obey anyone," until I made myself get up and shut the door. At that, he would run and jump on his bed, but as soon as I fell asleep again, he would sneak back through the dark and open my door. Sometimes this went on for hours. Looking back, I don't know why I didn't kill him—except that God had his hand on us both.

Every morning I woke up tired. Tony was tired too, of course. I dressed and put on my now-fading smile along with my makeup. I couldn't bring myself to talk about my awful secret, so when asked, I pretended that everything was okay at home.

But the terrible stress was beginning to cause my physical

and mental health to deteriorate; my stuttering became so pronounced that I was embarrassed to talk. Some days I made it to my classes and managed to teach, but other days my wonderful teaching aide, Karen, would have to take over. In my office stacks of memos piled up unanswered; I just stared at them, unable to force myself out of my stupor. Making a simple phone call seemed like a gigantic hurdle. Often I left my desk and wandered aimlessly around campus—just to escape.

I lost my ability to concentrate. After faculty meetings I couldn't remember a thing that had taken place. If I needed a pencil and opened the drawer to get it, I would end up staring at the drawer until something startled me out of my trance. My life had become a blur; all my days just ran together, and I never knew whether it was Tuesday or Friday.

One day a meeting kept me later than usual, and Tony was home sitting at the table when I walked in. He seemed to wear a permanent frown these days, and his eyes were dull and lifeless.

Trying to be pleasant, I greeted him, "Hi, Tony, how was school?"

"I hate school!"

Okay, I thought to myself, I won't rise to the bait. I'll just fix dinner. Tony likes hamburgers. I'll make something that will make him happy. I had to coax myself into each move. Now, get the meat out, Carolyn. Now get out a plate. Better start the barbecue. It took every ounce of my energy to concentrate.

Pretty soon Tony said, "What's for dinner?"

"Barbecued hamburgers."

"I don't want hamburgers."

The meal was nearly ready. "I'm sorry, Tony, if you wanted something else you should have asked me before I started fixing hamburgers.

"I don't want hamburgers," he repeated sullenly.

"We're having hamburgers. If you don't want them, you don't have to eat." *You can starve,* I wanted to say.

We ate thick, juicy hamburgers in boring silence. They might just as well have been cardboard.

"Tony, how's Mrs. Spurling?"

He shrugged his shoulders—so much for conversation.

After dinner, to my amazement, Tony got up and helped me clear the table. Then he sat down at the table again, looking angry and drained. He probably felt the strain as much as I did.

"Mom," Tony spoke harshly, "Do I have to go to school? I hate it!"

I'd been hanging up a hand towel when Tony spoke, and it fell to the floor and stayed there. I couldn't bring myself to respond to his questions. We had been over the issue dozens of times. What more was there to say?

All of a sudden, my mind started racing, and the things that I wanted to say were awful. Faster and faster, my thoughts went wild! My body began to tremble and I held on to the towel rod for support while Tony's voice droned on about school in the background. A darkness seemed to be closing in around me and I imagined that the ceiling was slowly moving down to crush me. It was so heavy and so dark—I had to escape. Leaning on the refrigerator for support, then the doorway, then the wall, I managed to get into the bathroom and lock the door.

I finally found the switch, the light came on, and the fan began its loud whirring. Shaking even more now, I leaned up against the sink. Slowly I looked up at my reflection in the mirror. Emotions welled up in my body and I could hold in the flood no longer.

"God," I bellowed, "What have you done to me? I asked you to change my life, not ruin it. You're destroying me." The pain and anger spewed out, making me feel old and ugly. "You gave me a son and I can't even stand to be in the same room with him. It's not fair!"

Tears began to stream down my face. So very angry and so very tired, I cried without restraint for what seemed an eternity.

If God doesn't care, why should I? I can't take it anymore! I quit! I've had it and I want out! I hate it, God. I hate it. Nothing about my life is right anymore. I'll quit my job and disappear. No one will ever find me. I'll sell the house and leave—go to Washington or Oregon—anywhere!

What about Tony? a voice within me asked. You can't just dump him.

I was so tired, so confused. I'd take Tony with me—maybe I could find someone who'd want him. I cried all over again as I remembered the prediction of my failure: "You'll dump him in a year!"

The escape became a detailed plan in my mind. I had to start packing, but the sobs continued to well up from deep inside me and overflow again and again.

"God, you've always helped me," I cried, "and I've been faithful to you. Why are you destroying me now? I'm a failure and it's your fault! I give up! I quit!"

As I finally quieted, my will collapsed. It had always been strong; this was the first time in my life I had given up. As my will came crashing down, a little, limp, pathetic me, totally vulnerable, remained—and God's mighty arms were there to catch me. What a shock to find God at the end of my broken will.

His comforting spirit was so tangible, so real, that I hardly dared to breathe. I felt myself a disciplined child gathered gently into the restorative arms of a loving parent. I was ready to listen and he was ready to talk.

Looking in the mirror again, I saw past my reflection into my own childhood. Remembrances—so vivid I could smell, feel, taste, them—stabbed at my heart. Why was this happening? I rarely looked back at my childhood. I had intentionally walked away from all that ugliness; it was irrelevant to my life today. But there it was, my own past, flashing before my eyes in the mirror, as if I were drowning. It was eerie!

The things stored in the huge trunk at the foot of my bed were not mine, but, reasoning like any eight-year-old, I decided to look inside anyway. After all, it **was** *in my bedroom. Under a stack of soft blankets my fingers discovered something hard and cold. I pulled it out —a real gun! Quickly I put it back and went outside to find my friend, Warren. We sneaked back to my room. Carefully, I shut the door tight and dug out the gun.*

"Look, Warren, it's real."

Warren was already my friend, but now he would really admire me. I had a real gun in my room.

"Carolyn," he whispered, "do you think it's loaded?" His eyes grew huge.

I pointed to the bullets in the chamber. "Sure it's loaded. Look here —"

The door flew open and my mother, seeing the gun, burst into the room and grabbed it, angrier than I had ever seen her. She pointed the gun straight at me, only inches from my face. Her finger was on the trigger.

"Where did you find this?" she demanded. "Tell me, where?" Both her voice and her hands shook with rage.

I pointed at the trunk, its lid hanging open.

"You better put it back and never touch it again. This is your dad's gun, and he hates your guts," she hissed. "One of these days he's going to kill you with it! You'd better pray that he dies before I do. I'm the only thing that keeps him from killing you now!"

Horror rippled across my mirrored reflection; the traumatic moment so long ago was still very painful. My dad had never been affectionate, but why had he hated me so?

Then I remembered Tony's dad and how he had beaten him with a chain. I knew exactly how he felt.

More of my past forced its way into my mind. When we drove from Montana to California with all our belongings in a panel truck and a trailer, I was forced to sit on a piano bench the entire time. For three days and nights I sat on that hard, cold bench while my two brothers stretched out comfortably on mattresses or sat in the front with my parents. Out of treatment like this, I gradually hardened myself to rejection and developed a survival ethic.

A survival ethic . . . I was snapped back to the present. Suddenly it was Tony's face I saw in the mirror, not mine. He was a survivor too!

After the experience on the piano bench I had begun to notice that my dad never looked at me or spoke to me unless he was angry. For some reason, no one in our family talked to me very much. In fact, I couldn't really remember any fun times with my family; we rarely even celebrated Christmas or birthdays.

I was really surprised when my father came home with bicycles for each of my brothers on their birthdays, beautiful, brand-new bicycles. I'd never seen anything like them. As my own birthday drew near I begged my father for a bicycle, too.

At last the big day arrived. My father backed his old red pickup into the driveway, and my heart stood still.

As he looked down at me from the bed of the truck, he said, "I stopped at the junkyard today and got the bike you've been begging me for."

He picked up the bike, handlebars rusted, tires flat, the blue paint chipped away. "There's your damn bicycle," he said and threw it on the grass. "Don't ever ask me for anything else as long as you live."

Apparently, I was in trouble again. Why, I didn't know. But it didn't matter, I had my very own bicycle. Taking it into the garage, I grabbed a wrench and tore it down. Soon the rust was mostly gone, the tires were repaired, and it glistened with a new coat of the paint I found on the shelf. I was so proud as I rode down the street, the wind blowing in my face and whipping my hair back! What a feeling to be riding my very own bike!

It was trucklike and hard to peddle, but I was determined to handle it. Wheeling it into the driveway, I lined it up right beside my brothers' bicycles. Then, through the screen door, I saw my family sitting around the table with soft drinks, having forgotten all about me.

This is my chance, I thought. I jumped on my brother's new Schwinn and flew down the street like a jet. Faster and faster, how easily it peddled. What a great bike! Quickly I returned it and took *a ride on my other brother's bike, a three-speed with real gears. It was simply wonderful—like riding on a cloud. My heart hammered as I returned, but I managed to park it without being caught and just stood there looking at the three birthday gifts from our dad. Voices and laughter still came from inside the house.*

A sorrowful feeling settled over me as I began to wonder if my family had little use for me. I remember, right then and there, making a decision: "If I'm going to make it, I'm going to make it myself. I don't need anyone!" And I never did ask them for anything again. Not even love!

I did make it, too! If I wanted something, I just stole it and told my mom it belonged to a friend. My way was not wise, and I suffered by making the poor choices my empty heart drove me to, year after year.

"I don't need anyone. I can make it myself." The words poured out of my mouth. I was saying them again, and how like Tony I sounded!

I stood there, still staring into the mirror. "Carolyn, you are just where I want you," the spirit of God seemed to be saying. "Tony has forced you to look at your past and remember how I took you through it and gave you a new life. Now you can show him how he can make it, too. I'm going to do the same thing for Tony that I have done for you. Be patient, Carolyn, and show him the way."

Tony was like me. What an incredible thought. He was more like me than if I had given birth to him myself. It wasn't an accident that he was my son, it was a well-executed miracle of God himself. Not only Tony's life, but his attitude paralleled mine in an uncanny way. God had brought us together, seemingly the most unlikely combination of mother and son, and now I was beginning to understand his purpose.

Tears ran down my face again, only this time they were tears of gratitude for all that God had done in my life and all he was doing in Tony's life.

It was difficult to estimate how long I had been in the bathroom. I washed my face and opened the door, not knowing if Tony would be there or not. As I rounded the corner of the kitchen, I saw that he sat at the table exactly where he had been when I left. He was wide-eyed and aware that something pretty serious was happening. It was out of character for me to disappear into the bathroom and come out tear-streaked.

Pulling the chair out, I seated myself across from him at the table. With a new understanding and commitment, I looked into his eyes and reached for his hand, enclosing it between mine.

"We're going to make it, Tony. We're going to make it, okay?" I said, squeezing his hand.

"Okay, Mom," he returned my squeeze.

Chapter Twenty-Four

In spite of my renewed understanding of and commitment to Tony, in spite of my growing trust in God, the days that followed were overwhelming. Two things had not changed: physically I was exhausted almost to the point of breakdown, and the conflicts with Tony, though less intense, continued.

But gradually our days began to look a little brighter. Tony showed signs of trying harder, but I was the one who had truly changed. I prayed that Tony, too, would soon see God's hand in his life.

He wasn't out to prove how bad he was anymore, but there were days of terrible moodiness. Knowing how close I had come to quitting on Tony, I was afraid that Tony might give up on himself—run away. When it seemed he just couldn't hack it anymore, I tried to encourage him. "It's okay, Tony, give yourself a chance. I made it, and so will you. I'll be here for as long as it takes; I'm willing to wait for you."

Some days he seemed to just crave another person's understanding and love, and I so badly wanted to be that person. As a child, day after day I had cried to myself, "Isn't there anybody who cares? Isn't there anybody who can show me how to be good?"

Even though his progress was slow, Tony did seem a little better adjusted each week. Some days he even seemed lighthearted, which filled me with joy.

Periodically little Donny would stop by to play with Tony. Donny was fun; he was always welcome. One day the boys wanted me to take them to a special movie, one they'd been talking about for weeks.

"Okay, guys, if you'll play nicely this morning and let me get my work done, I'll take you to the show."

"Yippee," they screamed, as they ran to get their kites

from the closet. "We're going to my old school, Mom," Tony called.

"Fine, be home by lunchtime. Donny can have lunch with us, and then we'll go to the show."

I buzzed around the house and cleaned like a beaver.

At about eleven, the door banged open and the boys flew past me up the stairs and into Tony's room, slamming the door behind them. Nothing's wrong, I told myself, keep sweeping. Whatever they were doing, it was very quiet. Soon I heard Tony's door open and close. I went on sweeping the floor.

"He didn't mean to do it," Donny's frantic whisper came from the living room.

I peeked around the corner, "What do you mean he didn't mean to do it? He didn't mean to do *what?*"

"Nothing, nothing. Oh, I wasn't supposed to tell! He didn't do it! It was an accident!"

One thing I'll say for Donny, he kept me informed; he couldn't keep anything a secret. *"What* was an accident?"

"He didn't mean to hit her! He didn't! He only sort of touched her."

By now I was really concerned. "What happened, Donny?"

"He just sort of pushed her," Donny whispered, and threw his arm toward my face to demonstrate.

I could see Tony creeping down the staircase trying to hear what Donny was saying.

"You know that girl who used to tease Tony at school?" Donny asked. "Well, she was over at the playground and started in again." I figured if I waited long enough, Donny would spill the whole story. "He just kind of pushed her. He didn't really mean to hurt her."

I could see Tony starting back up the stairs. "Tony, get down here," I yelled. "I want to talk to you." He turned slowly around and walked down the stairs looking very guilty.

"Sit down at the table, both of you. I want to know exactly what happened."

"I didn't hit her," Tony said. "I just pushed her."

"Yeah, but she ran home crying," Donny added helpfully.

"Tony, what happened?" I asked firmly.

"He hit her, he really hit her. But it didn't hurt her very much. She deserved it; she picked on him all last year." Poor Tony. Donny had blabbed the whole story.

"You mean you hit a girl, Tony?"

"Well, it wasn't too hard," Donny said.

Tony looked down. "Tony, did you hit a girl?" I asked, my outrage growing.

"N-n-n-n-no!" he stuttered.

"Don't lie, Tony. Did you hit a girl?"

"Yes!" he confessed.

Cultural differences or no, he should have known better. "Tony, boys don't go around hitting girls."

"Well, she used to pick on me all the time!"

"I don't care *what* she used to do, Tony. You shouldn't have hit her!" I was infuriated that my son had bullied a girl. I couldn't believe he'd done it! I tried to maintain my cool, but, for a moment I contemplated spanking both of them.

"Well, fellows, we won't be going to the show today. Tony, you're on restriction. I'm sorry Donny, you better—" Before I could finish, Tony exploded. He stood up, knocking over his chair, and ran into the dining area, where he had carefully laid out his electric train. He picked up the engine, pulled his arm back, and threw it all the way across the living room, smashing it into dozens of pieces and gouging a hole in the wall.

"You don't love me," he screamed. "You don't. You hate me." He spun around and with both arms viciously knocked the rest of the train layout across the room. "You don't love me!" he yelled in a rage and ran up the stairs to his room. "You hate me. You won't let me do anything!" I heard the door slam.

Donny's mouth was wide open. "I'm sorry, Donny, but you'll have to go."

"Okay, I'm going," he called, running out the door.

This was the last straw. Over the last year, I had heard

Tony yell, "You don't love me," too many times. It had always bugged me to hear a child say that to his parents. Now *I* was hearing it. The little ingrate.

I picked up an empty box from the garage and walked back into the living room. I glanced up to see Tony lying on the floor, peering through the banister at me. "You don't love me," he yelled. "You won't take me to the show. You don't love me. You make me stay home!"

Ignoring him, I picked up the pieces of the train. I took apart the track, section by section, dismantled the miniature telephone poles, and carefully packed everything into the box. Finally, I wrapped masking tape around it and took it to the garage.

When I came back into the house, I started up the stairs. Tony was horrified. His favorite toy had been packed away; he didn't know what would happen next. "You don't love me," he yelled, running into his room and slamming his door shut. I opened the door. He jumped from the floor to his bed, skittish as a wild cat. Was I going to spank him, or kill him? "You don't love me."

"Shut up, Tony."

"You said never to say 'shut up' and you said 'shut up,' " he reminded me.

"You're right, Tony. *Shut up!*" I sat down on a chair across the room from him.

"You won't take me to the show. You promised to take me to the show."

"I don't want to hear another word out of you, Tony."

"You said you would take us to the show. You promised."

"Tony, *not another word.*"

"You don't love me." Now he was whining.

"Tony," I pointed my finger at him. Finally he stopped. "I want to tell you something, Tony. I am sick and tired of you saying that I don't love you." He opened his mouth to speak, but I held my hand up to stop him. "Do you hear what I said, Tony? I am sick and tired of it. Tony, I want you to sit there and listen to everything I'm about to tell you and I don't want to hear another word from you until I'm done. Do you understand?''

He nodded his head.

"Tony, I'm going to tell you how much I love you in *your* terms for a change. I leaned forward and stared at him. "There is something I want to tell you that you need to hear." I paused impressively. "You know something, Tony, I don't *need* you." I let him agonize over that statement for a moment. I knew it was risky, but I believed this was the only way to make him understand me.

"Did you hear me?" His shocked face nodded yes.

"Tony, do you know what 'need' means?" I paused again, and he didn't move. " 'Need' means that you can't get along without something or someone, that you have to have it. Tony, I don't *need* you! But you know what? I *want* you! There's a big difference.

"You have to understand, Tony, I didn't adopt you to make me happy." He looked at me, listening carefully. "But, because I did adopt you, you have made me happy. Do you understand?" He lowered his eyes and nodded yes again.

"Tony, I am going to tell you how *much* I really love you. Do you have any idea what my life was like before I adopted you?" He looked a little nervous. "Do you realize that I was really very happy? I had it made. I had this nice house, a great job, lots of friends, all kinds of freedom. But, Tony, because I loved you so much, I adopted you, and you have made my life even fuller. I knew a lot of things would have to change when you became my son, but I was willing to change them because I love you.

"See this beautiful home?" He nodded, wondering where I was headed. "Tony, I had this whole house all to myself. It was great. It was easy to clean. In fact, I didn't have to clean it very often because I rarely got it dirty. Your room was the guest room; I could have people over whenever I wanted. But I loved you so much that I wanted you to live here with me. I wanted this to be your house, too. Now I clean this house far more than I ever did, because I love you.

"I used to have total freedom. I never had to come home after work and I could be gone most weekends. After work, if I wanted to go visit friends, I'd go. If I wanted to go to the show or out to dinner, I'd go. But I loved you so much that I gave up my freedom for you! I come home every day at three-fifteen to be with you. And it's worth it, Tony, because I love you so much.

"You know, Tony, as I look back over the last couple of years, I realize I had to give up a lot for you, but I love you so much that I would do it again and again and again. I have given you myself, I have given you my house, I have given you my time, I have given you my freedom. I have given you all that I can give you."

Tears were beginning to trickle down my son's face. He understood exactly what I was saying.

I moved to the foot of his bed and gently took his hand. "Now, Tony, please look at me. It seems that I have been doing all the giving and you have been doing all the receiving. I want to tell you something. In order for us to make it as mother and son, we *both* have to give. Tony, I have a lot to learn about being a mother. I know that I have failed in many ways with you, and I'm sorry, but I've never been a mother before, and it's not easy. I don't think that you have ever really been a son before either, and that's tough, too. But we can learn together. Tony, son, starting now, I want to try to out-give you and I want you to try and outgive me. And, I don't ever, *ever,* want to hear you say, 'You don't love me,' because I *do;* I love you very, very much."

By now I was crying, too. It had been hard for me to explain my love to Tony, but it was probably the first time he understood what it meant for me to love him. He reached his arms out, and we hugged each other. "I love you, Tony."

"I love you, Mom," he sobbed. "I will fix that train, okay?"

I smiled and hugged him. We were back on the right road, ready to continue our journey.

Chapter Twenty-Five

When Tony finally believed that I loved him and would never leave him, he relaxed and stopped struggling. Somehow his confidence in our relationship enabled him to listen and reason much more clearly.

He still disliked school very much but endured it until the year was over. And the school endured him, although Mr. Cook suggested he might be better off elsewhere in the fall. I agreed: Tony needed a fresh start once again. Starting over in another school would be easier than living down the bad reputation he had gained at this one—the kid who always got in fights and who'd even pulled a knife on a teacher. Tony's only regret was leaving his friend and ally, Mrs. Spurling.

As soon as summer vacation was upon us, Tony and I packed our bags and headed for the mountains for a couple of weeks with Grandma and Grandpa Peters. We were ready for a break.

The mountain air refreshed me immediately. "It feels so good to be here, Alva," I said, helping myself to more coffee cake at our first morning's breakfast.

"More coffee, Carolyn?" Alva urged.

"Yes, thanks." The steaming brew tasted like heaven. "What's on the agenda for today?"

"Well, I thought you might like the day off, but I do have some plans for Tony."

"What, Grandma, what?" Tony asked eagerly.

"There's a special teacher . . ."

"Oh no," he groaned.

"Now wait a minute. It's not what you think. Mrs. Dilgard has lots of games she plays with her students. She's more than a teacher anyway; she's my friend, and I would like you to meet her, Tony."

As it turned out, Sally Dilgard was a highly trained bilingual/cross-cultural specialist in her mid-forties who dealt specifically with reading problems. She had also had some training in working with stutterers. Like Mrs. Spurling, she was warm and easygoing. A lot of the kids in our extended family went to Mother Lode Christian School, so Tony seemed eager to go over there and see them and Mrs. Dilgard.

Tony came home from his first visit talking a mile a minute about what Mrs. Dilgard had taught him that day. "I even jumped on a trampoline and learned about stuttering. Mom, Mrs. Dilgard knows how to make me learn! She says she can teach me to read!"

Sally Dilgard came to talk with me one afternoon. "I've been testing Tony and he's reading at the third-grade level. Does that sound about right to you?"

"Yes, Sally. But he's been at that same level for a year."

"Oh, that's surprising. You know, Tony is very bright!"

"I know, but school's been very tough for him," I explained. Making social and emotional adjustments has taken so much out of him he's not had much left for academics."

"Carolyn, if I could work with Tony for a year here at school, I think we could get him off this plateau he seems stuck on."

"You're probably right, Sally, but I teach in the Los Angeles area. It would be impossible for me to live here for a year."

Alva had already mentioned this to me and couldn't wait to jump in with some help. "But Carolyn, lots of people would love to keep Tony for the school year. Why don't you let us help him and you?"

"Thanks, but I could never leave Tony. We're too close, and even if I wanted to, he would refuse."

"Well," Sally began, "why don't you think about it and pray about it and let us know later."

Back home in Glendora I thought about Alva and Sally's suggestion. I looked into schools for Tony in our area but found none that offered a reading program suited to his needs.

Nonetheless, I called Alva and told her I'd decided against Mother Lode Christian School.

"I simply can't suggest to Tony that he live with someone else for a while, even if it's only while school's in session. As far as I'm concerned, it would be better for him to never read well than to feel that I was rejecting him. He's had enough rejection!"

Everyone in the mountains was really disappointed. Apparently they had been talking about it a lot. Some close friends who already had five children even committed themselves to taking him. Their willingness and love for Tony impressed me deeply.

The previous semester, the director of our graduate program in education had approached me about a special teaching opportunity in the summer. He wanted me to teach a graduate course, Effective Teaching, to missionaries on study leave. It would be offered through the university's Operation Impact program and would mean a month's teaching tour through New Guinea, Taiwan, and the Philippines.

"I would love it and love the break, but I just couldn't. What would I do with Tony?"

Sonja, my secretary, had spoken up. "Maybe Michael and I could take care of him? Why don't I check with him before you turn down the job?"

If ever my mouth fell open, it was then. Sonja had been my secretary since before I became a mother. If anyone knew what she was getting into, it was Sonja.

I left on the teaching tour right after Tony and I returned from our visit to the mountains. Tony loved Sonja and her husband, Michael. They were young, practically newlyweds, and I reasoned they could take anything for a month!

This, the first extra speaking or teaching I had done in two years, stimulated and renewed me. When I returned, Sonja and Michael were graciously quiet about their month with Tony, except to tell me that Tony had taken my car keys and demonstrated his driving skills to Donny. They wouldn't have bothered me with that trivia, but Tony had pretty well demolished the new freezer standing in the far end of our garage.

During my tour, I had given Tony's schooling a lot more thought. The summer was half over and I hadn't found the right school. Although I remained unwilling to send Tony away to school, I couldn't help feeling Mother Lode would be good for him. I also remembered a conversation I had had with Ron Cline in Mexicali that first year after I had adopted Tony.

"Carolyn, as a single parent, you might not like my next suggestion, but I do want you to think about it. Tony doesn't know much about family life. He's never seen how a healthy family functions together. He needs the opportunity to see how a married couple interacts, how a man relates to a wife and children in the context of a two-parent family. Sometime before he graduates from high school, try to have him live for a time with a family—for his sake."

What Ron had said made sense. I called my friend Norm Wright, a marriage and family counselor, to see what he thought. "I agree very strongly with Ron about putting Tony in a family situation sometime before he graduates. But you're right, too, rejection could be a problem; maybe it's not the right time yet."

It hurt a bit to have Tony's and my relationship excepted from the concept "whole-family," but I understood what Ron and Norm meant. There was a built-in disadvantage to single parenting.

Norm's final words of advice that day were probably the best I had received. "Remember, Carolyn, because Tony has an unusual background, he will require some unusual parenting techniques. Try to make every decision based on what's best for Tony rather than what's accepted as best for the "normal" middle-class American youngster. And be prepared for criticism!"

I was pulled so strongly in so many directions that I simply could not make a decision. I left it in God's hands. "Lord, I want to thank you for bringing Tony into my life. I love him so much. Please help me to know what to do about school. If it would be best for Tony to go to school in the mountains this year, let him ask me if he can go. That way, Lord, I'll know he won't feel rejected."

Several weeks passed. I was standing at the kitchen sink preparing lunch one Sunday after church when Tony floated into the room. "God really loves me, doesn't he, Mom?"

I gave him a mustard-drenched squeeze. "He sure does, Tony!"

"I'm a pretty lucky boy, aren't I, Mom?"

"You're very lucky, son, and very special too." I winked at him, feeling puffed up with contentment. He walked over to the table and sat down.

"Mom?"

"Yes, Tony."

"I've been thinking . . ." He sounded serious, so I wiped my hands and joined him at the table. "I really messed up at my first school, and then at my second school, too."

I had to agree. "But you learned a lot, Tony. We knew it wouldn't be easy."

"Well, do you think I could go to school in the mountains? Mrs. Dilgard is a good teacher, and I think she could teach me how to read."

I couldn't believe my ears. Those were exactly the words I had told God I needed to hear. That was an answer from God.

We talked about the decision for hours that day and often in the days that followed. Several times Tony changed his mind. But in the end, moving to the mountains was Tony's choice. We both knew it would be terribly painful to be separated just as our love for each other was becoming so incredibly strong, but it wouldn't be forever. I was now truly his mother and he was my son.

It wasn't just a couple of people from the Peterses' church that encouraged us; the entire congregation was behind us. A tremendous family of friends surrounded and encouraged us, especially John and Ann Magwood and their five children, who opened their home to Tony.

With the Magwoods, Tony saw family life as it should be

lived. John and Ann related well to each other and to their children. All the children had chores every day: cleaning, hauling wood, and so on, but it seemed natural to work together as a part of the family—and fun, too. Tony joined right in, even learning some basic cooking skills. After dinner each night they all prayed together and read from the Bible, then enjoyed playing some games or doing homework.

Tony and I talked for hours on the telephone regularly. Some weeks we talked every night. I was definitely "Mom" and Tony called me every time he faced a decision. I talked with the Magwoods often, too, and with Tony's principal and teachers, many of whom were my former students or old friends from Mexicali Outreach. Tony still had difficulties to work out, but all reports were encouraging. He was making real progress not only academically but socially; he played soccer and basketball and even sang in the school choir.

As often as possible I drove up to see him and meet with his many guardians and teachers. Each visit became an excuse to have a "family" dinner, which Tony dearly loved. Often he was able to catch a ride down the mountain and come home for the weekend, and we somehow managed to stretch each school holiday to its maximum number of days out of school. All in all we saw quite a lot of each other that school year.

When Paul Taylor called and asked me to be the commencement speaker at Tony's eighth-grade graduation I laughed out loud.

"What's so funny?" Paul asked.

"Oh, it's just a shock to have Tony's principal call for something other than a discipline problem."

"Tony's done very well, and he's graduating. It would really mean a lot to him for you to be our speaker. Besides, the senior class is graduating at the same time, and they suggested you for their speaker."

"I would consider it an honor to be your graduation speaker," I said, pleased and proud. I had never spoken at a graduation before, and this was my son's!

I arrived at the auditorium early, but already it was filling up with excited family members and friends. The graduates scurried around in excitement—eighth-graders in their brand-new suits and dresses, seniors in their graduation gowns. I glanced down over the crowd, looking for Tony. There he was, the best-looking eighth-grader in the group—to his mother, at least! He was beaming from ear to ear. If he wasn't careful, he'd burst the buttons on his vest.

Paul Taylor spotted me and began to explain the program. "By the way," he said, "Tony came into my office a couple of days ago and asked if he could say a few words to the audience before you speak."

Had I misunderstood? "Tony wants to speak in front of the whole audience?" My mind flashed back over the last two years. Tony's teachers could hardly get him to speak out even in small groups of three or four, partly because of the stuttering problem.

Mr. Heath, the superintendent, joined us; both men were grinning from ear to ear. "Apparently he really wants to!" they said. "And we told him he could." By now they were both laughing at my shock.

"Well, what does he want to say?"

"We don't know, we didn't ask him."

I looked at them in pure astonishment. My son was going to stand up and speak in front of the graduation class—they had given him permission to do it—and they didn't even know what he was going to say. This should be some graduation, I thought to myself.

As I sat on the platform I looked at my son, so handsome in his first three-piece suit. Tony grinned with delight as we looked across the stage at each other.

Then Mr. Taylor invited Tony to the podium. "Tony would like to say a few words before his mother comes up to speak." I glanced over at Tony. He looked somehow both confident and terrified. He grabbed the podium with both hands, then relaxed a bit and shoved one hand into his pocket. When he opened his mouth to speak, he couldn't get past his stutter, but he was determined and began again.

"I want to thank this school for what they have done for me!" Then he turned sideways. "And I want to thank my mom for adopting me and bringing me here to the United States. It's the greatest thing that ever happened in my life." He turned to face me. Tears streaming down his face, he yelled, "I love you, Mom. I love you. I love you!" as if wanting the whole world to hear. He threw his arms around me and cried again, "Mom, I love you, I love you!"

Overcome, I clung to him. "Tony, I love you, too." We held each other and sobbed, unaware of the hundreds of people—who by then were wiping the tears from their own eyes.

I left my carefully prepared speech on my chair and walked forward arm in arm with my son, Tony. Now it was my turn to cling to the podium. I stood there for a long time, unable to control my tears. I was years back in time, rehearsing all that God had taken us through and how he had changed our lives.

God had given Tony a mother and me a son, filled a void in my life that I hadn't even realized was there. Now every day was a challenge and alive with the fulfilling intimacy of a committed and loving relationship with another person.

Still fighting tears, I choked, "And now I'm supposed to give a graduation speech!"

Released from the tension of emotion, the audience exploded in thunderous applause and cheers.

At last I was able to speak. "God has performed a beautiful miracle in both our lives and taken us on an incredible journey! And it all started when I asked God to change my life. So I ask each of you today, have you ever asked God to change your life? I mean *really* change it! He will, and it will be worth it!"

Years of pain, disappointment, anger, doubt, and fear now were woven into a laurel of victory and joy: It had been worth it all to hear that healing balm of words, "Mom, I love you. I love you!"

Epilogue

It is amazing what the commitment of love will do to a relationship, whether it be the love between husband and wife, between friends, or between mother and son. Love heals wounds, erases scars, sets a foundation, and builds a future. Because of God's love, Tony's future is like a radiant, free light of God at the end of a dark tunnel.

Eighth-grade graduation was a victory not only for Tony but for everyone in his world. For a huge investment of love had flowed freely for many years to make it possible. As Tony continued his schooling, it was from a small but firm foundation that he took his next steps. He joined the soccer team his first semester (and spent most practices trying to imitate people). Second semester he played basketball. A big thrill for my deep-voiced son was getting into the school choir. "See that kid in the front row, the one with a shining, radiant tan face? The one right there in the front? With the special twinkle in his eyes? That's my son, Tony."

High school was a new experience: Soccer and basketball games, choir concerts, tours, musicfests, and school retreats. Mrs. Dilgard continued to work with Tony on his reading and English. His reading level improved so much that he was actually able to be in all the regular classes with his friends.

Tony rapidly improved in school but that doesn't mean our whole world turned around and there were no more problems. Tony was now a typical student and teenager; he needed more prodding to do homework, more discipline, and much more encouragement. But I marveled at his continued growth and his zest for life.

Most important of all, real bonding took place between us. As I have watched Tony mature and become all that God wants him to be, I have developed a real respect for him, for all that he has gone through in his life, for his fight for his own right to live.

Tony has now graduated from high school. It was a big year for my son. He was busily involved in all the exciting activities seniors get themselves into—high school athletic events, heavy schoolwork, concern about grades, senior pictures, school retreats, and girls, girls, and girls.

Tony has also been very active in the church youth program and has found real support among the young people there.

I still work full-time on the faculty at Azusa Pacific University and am also the executive director of our new Institute for Outreach Ministries. The whole Mexicali program has grown to such an extent that in 1984 there were three trips down to Mexico. Over two thousand high school and college students signed up for the Easter trip alone.

Tony has also become involved in the police department's high school cadet program—something that he not only loves but takes very seriously. As a cadet he wears his new police cadet uniform, attends weekly training meetings, goes on "ride-alongs" with patrolmen in their police cars, and assists with crowd control at parades and special functions.

"Mom, I might want to be a policeman. I want to help people and protect them. I think I can." I know you can, Tony, I know you can! I really believe Tony can help people. He seems to have an instinct for reaching out to someone who is hurting—someone who needs special help. We're not sure exactly what occupation Tony will choose. He is very gifted mechanically, works well with his hands—drawing, designing, doing woodwork and carpentry—and has a wonderful sensitivity to people. Whatever it is, God will use him.

When I discovered Tony, now over nine years ago, in that boys' prison in Mexico, little did I know that one day that special little boy with the twinkle in his eyes would change the rest of my life. Little did I know the pain and suffering I would go through—and how the wounds of my own past would be reopened to be dealt with once again. Little did I know the impact Tony—my son—would have on my life and on the lives of thousands. Little did I know of the special journey God had set out for us.

Within weeks of bringing Tony into the United States, I got calls from all over the country—friends, pastors, Christian magazines, and book publishers—to put our story in writing. These people all encouraged me to write for the sake of the many thousands of hurting people who need to realize that no matter what personal prison they have in their own past, what hell they are living in now, God does care and will reach down and put their lives together and love and care for them just as he has done in our lives. God has a special journey for them, too!

My response to these requests was, "No, we're not ready for that." Even Tony heard about the many requests to put our story in writing: "You going to write a book about us, Mom?"

"I don't know, Tony. At least not for a long time. I didn't adopt you to write a book. I adopted you because God gave me a special love for you, and God has a lot of things he wants to do in our lives before we can tell our story. We don't have to worry about it. If and when it's time to write a book and tell others about our journey, we will know. We will feel real peace about it."

The years passed without further mention of a book. The journey was hard, but the exciting thing about a journey is that it never ends—it's as if it's just begun.

A little over a year ago, on a warm summer evening, I was standing in the kitchen preparing dinner. I saw Tony ride his bike in front of the house into the garage. Within seconds he crashed through the front door and into the kitchen, throwing his arms around me.

"Hi, Mom!"

"Hi, sweets." I returned his hug.

"You know, Mom, I've been thinking about something," he continued.

"What's that, Tony?"

"You can write that book now! I'm doing okay, aren't I?"

A sudden spark of mutual affirmation shot through us as we stood there in our cozy kitchen. We both sensed that each of us was ready.

"You know something, Tony? You're right! You're absolutely right. I can write that book now!"